# THE JANUS OF POETS

## CAMBRIDGE
### UNIVERSITY PRESS

University Printing House, Cambridge CB2 8BS, United Kingdom

Cambridge University Press is part of the University of Cambridge.

It furthers the University's mission by disseminating knowledge in the pursuit of education, learning and research at the highest international levels of excellence.

www.cambridge.org
Information on this title: www.cambridge.org/9781107432130

© Cambridge University Press 1935

First published 1935
First paperback edition 2014

*A catalogue record for this publication is available from the British Library*

ISBN 978-1-107-43213-0 Paperback

# THE JANUS OF POETS

Being an essay on the
Dramatic Value of Shakspere's Poetry
both good and bad

by

RICHARD DAVID

*Scholar of Corpus Christi College*
*Cambridge*

The very Janus of poets; he wears almost everywhere
two faces; and you have scarce begun to admire the one,
ere you despise the other.                    DRYDEN

CAMBRIDGE
AT THE UNIVERSITY PRESS
1935

# NOTE

The first two of the following Parts, together with a very rough draft of the third, formed the Harness Prize Essay for 1934. My thanks are due to the Awarders for permission to expand and re-organise the whole before publication.

# CONTENTS

# INTRODUCTION

THIS is an attempt to discover exactly what Shakspere, as a *dramatic poet*, was doing, and how he came to do it.

These particular questions are part of a general problem: what are the advantages and disadvantages accepted by the dramatist who writes his plays in verse, and the poet who chooses the dramatic form as the shape in which to cast his imaginings? This larger question has already been answered by two poets, one of whom was himself a dramatist, the other believed that he possessed "a turn for philosophical criticism, and especially for insight into the genius of Shakespere".

There are, according to Coleridge,

two legitimate conditions which the critic is entitled to expect in every metrical work. First, that as the elements of metre owe their existence to a state of increased excitement, so the metre itself should be accompanied by the natural language of excitement. Secondly, that as these elements are formed into metre artificially, by a voluntary act, with the design and for the purpose of blending delight with emotion, so the traces of present volition should throughout the metrical language be proportionately discernible.

It is unfortunate that no Skionar is a greater caricature of Coleridge, than is Coleridge himself. His philosophical jargon often obscures his naturally sound and straightforward sense, and even when the meaning has been properly understood the reader may doubt his understanding. The present passage, for all its practical application, is especially teasing, because in it the author seems to be stating, as parallels, two results of writing in verse which are not strictly so. His first condition is the well-known effect which poetry possesses, of raising thought or emotion to a higher pitch of intensity, of universalising them, of making them more than human. The second appears to be a different kind of condition: it is the disarming of the obvious layman's criticism—"Verse-speech is not life-like"; to which the answer is that the artificiality of verse is deliberately encouraged by the dramatic poet as an essential factor in the creation of that ideal world, "avoiding and excluding all accident", in which a dramatic action is set to greatest effect.

Whatever the intention of Coleridge's original, there is here extracted from it a concise account of the dramatist's final aim in writing in verse, and of the method of writing verse by which he attains that aim. Coleridge perhaps too much assimilates the method to the aim. Dryden may be thought to err in the other direction; his interest in the technical side of the problem leads him to treat the aim often as no more than a mere incident to the method. This is his answer to the question, as given in the Defence of his Essay of Dramatick Poesy:

To affect the soul, and excite the passions, and, above all, to move admiration (which is the delight of serious plays), a base imitation will not serve. The converse, therefore, which a poet is to imitate, must be heightened with all the arts and ornaments of poesy: and must be such as, strictly considered, could never be supposed spoken by any without premeditation.

Or, more particularly, in the Essay itself:

Verse, 'tis true, is not the effect of sudden thought; but this hinders not that sudden thought may be represented in verse, since those thoughts must be higher than Nature can raise them without premeditation, especially to a continuance of them, even out of verse; and consequently you cannot imagine them to have been sudden either in the poet or in the actors.

The dramatist, then, who writes in verse, is accepting a convention, but one which properly used is rather a help than a hindrance to the full expression he desires. His action takes place in a world which is not the everyday world; but in it all thought and emotion are as it were distilled, of greater chemical purity than those of the everyday world. This means, of course, that he has deliberately cut himself off from the realistic play, and perhaps also from that in which the delineation of character provides the chief interest. By writing in verse he has pledged himself to the serious play, in the Aristotelian sense; to a play in which πρᾶξις, action in its widest application—that is, the given tangle of interrelations with their overtones of emotion—is of primary importance. He has undertaken a piece of writing in which any lowering of intensity below a certain pitch is fatal. The play in verse, the action isolated in its universalised world, is more sustained, more of a piece, than the realistic play. There is no room for inessentials, nor for passages of padding such as are sometimes admissible, for instance, in the epic. The serious play needs a greater degree of concentration.

This last is a condition which the dramatic poet

feels more in his second character, that of poet
turned dramatist; and there are others which are
better considered from this point of view than
from its opposite. The poet who casts his work
in dramatic form is imposing upon himself an
additional restraint. It is possible to be too
poetical for drama. Of the Elizabethans, Marston was always too conscious of his high calling,
so that the more serious of his plays walk upon
literary stilts, and only *The Dutch Courtesan*, aim-
ing at low life, finds a dignified mean; Fletcher's
luxuriance can hardly be kneaded into any
dramatic shape; and even Shakspere, at least in
his early plays, may sometimes be accused of
prolonging his lyricism further than the situation
gives any warrant for. But this additional restraint is counterbalanced by the vastly increased
range of expression which a dramatic form lends
to poetry. The same phrase will vary immensely
in its emotional force according to the character
and situation to which it is assigned; and the
dramatic poet can play the same melody, simple
or complex, with a wide variety of stops. His
compass too—at least in the case of the Elizabethans—is greatly increased; for the whole
gamut of language is at his disposal, from the

most colloquial prose to the most impassioned verse.

It is in the light of these conditions governing the work of a dramatic poet that I wish now to examine Shakspere's verse; to see how he met the advantages and disadvantages that a dramatic poet incurs, how he used poetry to aid his dramatisation and dramatic effect to aid his poetry; to judge, in short, how far this title of *dramatic poet* does indeed become him.

# *PART I*

## POETRY AND DRAMA

IT is perilously easy to think of a poet's artistic development not as a living growth, but as a tabulated sequence in a history book, in which each calculated event leads logically to its successor, and the stages are vividly distinguished. An artist's progress is nothing so deliberate and self-conscious; and all attempts to see it as such result—look at almost any critical study of Beethoven or Mozart—either in its crystallisation into a few grand periods with which the works obstinately refuse to correspond, or its resolution into as many phases and "manners" as there are opus numbers.

Such a treatment is even more misleading applied to a dramatist than to a musician. For the dramatist is concerned, technically, with the presentation of definite stage-effects, in the highest sense of the phrase; and to achieve them he will use any method that he has found successful, at whatever stage of his development he first conceived it. It is therefore impossible to fix and define Shakspere's technique at any one moment of his career, or to assign a play to an early date and immature practice simply on the ground, say, that certain scenes in it contain a large number of rhymed couplets; Shakspere was always prepared to write couplets if they would best effect his purpose.

Not that the dramatist necessarily thinks out the appropriate style of verse or prose for every mood, and then consciously employs each in its right place; to assume that is as serious a mistake as the other. It is more likely that he instinctively varies the tone-colour as the emotional atmosphere changes. But here again the business of playwriting is seen to be a very fluid thing, to which the rules of evidence and law-court procedure cannot be applied.

It will be most important to remember this caution in a later section, when dealing with the immense variety of verse-styles which Shakspere employs side by side in his mature plays. I insert it here to remind the reader that a poet's development is by no means such a direct affair as the critic, in searching for the chief influences and underlying impulses, is almost bound to make it. In pointing out what seems to be the main current, he disregards the innumerable eddies and backwashes which accompany it.

The attempt to distinguish Shakspere's first "periods" meets with even greater difficulties than such attempts usually do. About the order of composition of his early plays there can be no certainty; and the original problem is further complicated by the fact that more than one of them show signs of having undergone a drastic revision at a much later date than that of the first writing. There is, however, one common denominator discoverable for those plays which external evidence suggests are the earliest. The scheme and motive of them all is a poetical one; they are literary rather than dramatic; the form and turn of the phrases betray the fact that Shakspere was here setting down words which he saw written upon an ideal page rather than heard spoken by an ideal actor.

The plays which common sense would put first are the imitations, of the classics and of Marlowe: *Titus Andronicus* following Kyd and the Senecans, the *Henry VI* trilogy and its pendant *Richard III*, which copy the historical and semi-historical plays of Marlowe, Peele, and Greene, and *The Comedy of Errors* based on

[ 3 ]

Plautus. There is very little poetry, good poetry, in any of these; what there is belongs either to the heaven-battle-thunder-devils or the rose-lily-ivory-and-gold school—in short to the Senecans or to the Sonneteers. There is very little that is distinctive of Shakspere; which is perhaps the reason why such a jostling crowd of dramatists, besides Shakspere, have at various times been admitted to their authorship. Yet they are competently written examples of their different genres, and the basic model upon which Shakspere is to found his first variations.

The verse of these early plays is adequate to the straightforward effects which are required of it, but has as yet little flexibility or power of variation. That of the historical series is boxed off into compartments as regular and precise as the heroic couplet; such lines as these, of Joan la Pucelle, seem to fall naturally into pairs:

Dismay not (Princes) at this accident,
Nor grieve that *Roan* is so recovered:
Care is no cure, but rather corrosive,
For things that are not to be remedy'd.
Let frantic *Talbot* triumph for a while,
And like a Peacock sweepe along his tayle,
Wee'le pull his Plumes, and take away his Trayne,
If *Dolphin* and the rest will be but rul'd;

and in Gloucester's defence the regular service and return is even more noticeable:

> Vertue is choakt with foule Ambition,
> And Charitie chas'd hence by Rancours hand;
> Foule Subornation is predominant,
> And Equitie exil'd your Highnesse Land, etc.

where the rhyme emphasises the movement. Often, of course, this underlying couplet-rhythm breaks surface, and produces large patches of actual rhymed verse, as in the death scenes of Talbot and his son; island outcrops—single couplets, or groups of two or three—appear at frequent intervals, and for no obvious reason, throughout the blank verse scenes; and often, even when the rhyme does not follow immediately, its appearance a line or two later produces the same distinctive checking and clinching effect:

From off the gates of *Yorke*, fetch down that head,
Your Father's head, which *Clifford* placed there;
In stead whereof, let this supply the roome,
Measure for measure, must be answered.

Or, more blatantly:

I have no Brother, I am like no Brother:
And this word (Love) which Gray-beards call Divine,
Be resident in men like one another,
And not in me:

[ 5 ]

Such a haphazard, almost accidental, use of rhyme is avoided by Shakspere in later plays, where the more compact couplet is still employed to make a point or emphasise a moral.

The "couplet-movement", if I may call it so, is responsible for the very short wavelength of the verse in these early plays. The voice rises in one line, subsides in the next. The mechanical return of each second line cuts short any attempt at a sustained period or a carefully prepared crescendo; the climaxes are abrupt, and follow each other with perfect timing and regularity at two-line intervals. It is only when the couplets are forgotten, and Shakspere is deliberately echoing Marlowe, that any sort of freedom or expansion is possible. Talbot, as a warrior-hero, inherits a trick of Tamburlaine's voice if no more; and consequently the climax of a battle scene has often a new breadth and vigour. Other emotional turning-points sometimes receive the same treatment; York, in his last agony, can utter a denunciation against Queen Margaret, parts of which have quite the Marlovian swing and drive; and the noble scenes between Suffolk and the Queen culminate in that great descriptive speech, often taken by the disintegrators for the work of Marlowe himself, which preludes Suffolk's death and the end of an important stage in the history:

The gaudy blabbing and remorsefull day,
Is crept into the bosome of the Sea:
And now loud houling Wolves arouse the Jades
That dragge the Tragicke melancholy night;
Who with their drowsie, slow, and flagging wings
Cleape dead-men's graves, and from their misty Jawes
Breath foule contagious darknesse in the ayre: etc.

But such stuff as this is only a highly coloured patch in the general fabric of the play. Elsewhere the measured rise and fall persist, and, even in continuous speeches by a single character, there is an ever-present sense of question and answer, quip and repartee; so that a passage of genuine stichomuthia, such as that between Richard and Edward IV's queen, does not stand out at all strikingly from its surroundings, as it would in a later play.

In a lighter work, *The Comedy of Errors*, this rhythm is found less cramped. The verse is still built up of repetitive sections, but the intervals are now longer, of three or four lines, and the voice is able to wander a little further before drifting back upon itself. This creates a curiously sing-song movement, whose leisureliness is often emphasised by the "Kydian turns" which are almost its only ornament:

DUKE. But had he such a Chaine of thee, or no?
ANG. He had my Lord, and when he ran in heere,
These people saw the Chaine about his necke.
MERCH. Besides, I will be sworne these eares of
    mine
Heard you confesse you had the Chaine of him,
After you first forswore it on the Mart,
And thereupon I drew my sword on you,
And then you fled into this Abbey heere,
From whence I thinke you are come by Miracle.
EPH. ANT. I never came within these Abbey wals,
Nor ever didst thou draw thy sword on me:
I never saw the chaine, so helpe me heaven:
And this is false you burthen me withall.

Here there is more freedom than in the verse of the first historical plays; but even here there is not that full power and lack of constraint that is found in the blank verse of Marlowe. I suggest, very tentatively, that this rhythm too is under domination; that it is shaped by another metrical form, less curt and definitive than the couplet-pattern of the Senecans, but still more or less rigid; that it is a development of the old semi-regular metre, which still survives in other parts of this play, and also in *Love's Labour's Lost*—as these couplets of Dromio of Ephesus:

Say what you wil sir, but I know what I know,
That you beat me at the Mart I have your hand to show;
If my skin were parchment, and the blows you gave were ink,
Your owne hand-writing would tell you what I thinke.

These lines have also the couplet-form, but without the precision of the true couplet. They too follow the boomerang flight, spinning out and up, checking, and returning to the thrower's hand; but the check is not so abrupt, and the return more dilatory. And it is exactly this delayed come-back which distinguishes the blank verse of *The Comedy of Errors* from that of *Henry VI*. The proof no longer follows the proposition immediately; the periods of the *Comedy* fall on the ear almost like an Aristotelian syllogism: All beasts that part not the hoof are anathema to the Jews; the camel's hoof is not parted: therefore the camel is anathema to the Jews.

This possibility of a primitive origin for Shakspere's early blank verse suggests that he, like

Greene, had written plays in irregular verse, which, like Greene's, have since disappeared. But however that may be, the type persists throughout the plays of his youth, being still the standard verse in the purely narrative and plot-forwarding scenes of *Richard II*, and also in *The Two Gentlemen of Verona*.

*Richard II* presents the problem of two verse-styles, representing different stages of Shak-spere's development, found side by side in the same play. Again and again the working verse, of the *Errors* type, gives way to sudden flights of a poetry which is more mature than anything written at the time of the play's composition, or for some years after, and which must therefore belong to a later revision. There was in fact a long addition to the deposition scene printed in the third Quarto, of 1608; but this does not contain the most striking passages, and was probably omitted from the two earlier editions only in deference to a political censorship. The revision that added the great rhetorical passages was made at a much earlier date. Even in the play as first issued in 1597, there are speeches of the King which, in energy and in control of move-ment, are strangely out of keeping with the humdrum verse of the greater part of the play. Such are Richard's philosophisings over the dwindling of his army, and in prison, and the shorter, but no less fine address to the traitor Northumberland:

> Wee are amaz'd, and thus long have we stood
> To watch the fearefull bending of thy knee,
> Because we thought ourselfe thy lawfull King:
> And if we be, how dare thy joynts forget
> To pay their awfull dutie to our presence?
> If we be not, shew us the Hand of God,
> That hath dismiss'd us from our Stewardship,
> For well we know, no Hand of Blood and Bone
> Can gripe the sacred Handle of our Scepter,
> Unless he doe prophane, steale, or usurpe.
> And though you thinke, that all, as you have done,
> Have torne their Soules, by turning them from us,
> And we are barren, and bereft of Friends:
> Yet know, my Master, God Omnipotent,
> Is mustring in His Clouds, on our behalfe,
> Armies of Pestilence, and they shall strike
> Your Children yet unborne, and unbegot,
> That lift your Vassall Hands against my Head,
> And threat the Glory of my precious Crowne.

I quote at length, because only in a long passage can the new drive and staying power of the verse be fully observed. It is in these qualities, in what are usually called the architectonics of verse, in the knowledge of connection, paragraphing, and the sustained period, that Shakspere has made his advance. This speech of Richard's moves forward in great springing curves, like a suspension bridge, without having to sink a pile at every second or third line, as in the first histories.

There is still, however, an essentially literary flavour about this writing. The measured beat of such a line as:

And threat the Glory of my precious Crowne,

especially with the Folio capitals to emphasise it, looks better on paper than it sounds when spoken; and the line immediately before it, carefully balancing Hands against Head, is only one example of that antithesis, studied, assessed, and weighed to the least fraction, which is so common an ornament of these speeches, and whose intrinsic literariness is better seen in the pun-variant of an earlier line:

Have *torne* their Soules, by *turning* them from us.

More important, these speeches of the King are placed, and used, with literary, rather than dramatic, purpose. They are leisurely developments of a theme taken from the play, rather than in any way organic to the play. In that quoted above, the divine right of Kings, and the protection which Heaven affords them, are treated in full, the ideas following one another easily and logically. Compare with this a speech from *King Lear*, which may be said to approach the same subject from a more material and practical standpoint:

> EDM. Sir, I thought it fit
> To send the old and miserable King
> To some retention and appoynted guard;
> Whose age had Charmes in it, whose Title more,
> To plucke the common bosome on his side,
> And turne our imprest Launces in our eies
> Which do command them.

The rapidly shifting imagery, the mixed metaphors, give a sense of urgency to this passage, which Richard's speech has not, for all its rhetorical power. Shakspere has not yet learnt to concentrate his force. The Queen grieves for Richard's departure, and Bushy's comfort is as orderly and homiletic as a tract:

> Each substance of a greefe hath twenty shadows
> Which shewes like greefe it selfe, but is not so:
> For sorrowes eye, glazed with blinding teares,
> Divides one thing intire, to many objects,
> Like perspectives, which rightly gaz'd upon
> Shew nothing but confusion, ey'd awry

Distinguish forme: so your sweet Majestie
Looking awry upon your Lord's departure,
Finde shapes of greefe, more than himselfe to waile,
Which look'd on as it is, is naught but shadowes
Of what is not: then thrice-gracious Queen,
More then your Lord's departure weep not,
    more's not seene;
Or if it be, 'tis with false sorrowes eie,
Which for things true, weepe things imaginary.

He states the thought, develops it in a simile,
applies the simile closely, and draws the correct
conclusion. Something of the same thought,
when uttered by Macbeth, leaps to its conclusion
even as it develops:

                    Present Feares
Are lesse than horrible Imaginings.
My Thought, whose Murther yet is but fantasticall,
Shakes so my single state of Man, that Function
Is smothered in surmise, and nothing is
But what is not.

To return, these speeches of the King are really
no more than magnificent digressions, and have
no dramatic value, except in so far as they present
the essentially undramatic and digressive character of the speaker. That beginning "Let's talk of
Graves, of Wormes, and Epitaphs" provides of
course a good contrast to the dramatic succession

of bearers of ill news which has immediately preceded it, and well suggests the pit of dejection into which the King and his party are fallen; the long metaphysical soliloquy, "I have bin studying, how to compare This Prison where I live, unto the World", is appropriate to the prisoner and expressive of his state of mind. But all these poetic patches occur at moments of rest and not of action, either physical or spiritual; they present a state, do not reveal a growth. They are like the cadenzas in a concerto, where the soloist, taking a theme from the main work as his starting-point, expounds it and improvises upon it at his own free will, while the orchestra waits, inactive. So Richard philosophises, and the action of the play is suspended, awaiting his final trill.

The cadenzas, which I take to be late additions, are of a much higher order of verse than what may be called, by analogy, the "tutti passages" of the play. These are all of the sing-song pattern already studied in the earliest plays. Upon this *The Two Gentlemen of Verona* shows a definite advance. Here the verse has already begun to flow more easily and fully, besides being more picturesque and highly coloured; but the old movement can still be detected, especially when

in connection with the old device of the "turn".
A speech of Proteus provides a good example of
this, as well as of the new richness and elaboration:

VAL. Doth *Silvia* know that I am banish'd?
PRO. I, I; and she hath offered to the doome
(Which un-reverst stands in effectual force)
A Sea of melting pearle, which some call teares;
Those at her fathers churlish feete she tender'd,
With them upon her knees, her humble selfe,
Wringing her hands, whose whiteness so became
    them,
As if but now they waxed pale for woe:
But neither bended knees, pure hands held up,
Sad sighes, deepe grones, nor silver-shedding teares
Could penetrate her uncompassionate Sire.

Here the more decorative language and the
greater suppleness of the rhythm in individual
lines—for instance the picturesque onomato-
poeia of "Sad sighes, deepe grones, nor silver-
shedding teares"—connect the play with Shakspere's excursion into pure poetry. The influence
of his experiments is more clearly felt in the next
group of plays, in *Love's Labour's Lost*, in *Romeo
and Juliet*, and in *A Midsummer Night's Dream*.
In these appear not only Petrarchan phrases and
lyrical rhythms, but the actual forms of non-

[ 16 ]

dramatic verse, such as the sonnet, and the favourite sestet-stanza of *Venus and Adonis*; and with the last two plays at least, there comes a curious feeling that the action is being worked out at two levels—the purely dramatic one of the plot, and the poetic, hovering more indefinitely, like a sort of harmonic, above it. *Love's Labour's Lost*, being less of a coherent whole, does not produce quite the same effect. Whether we believe in a pre-Shaksperian state of this play or not, it is obvious, even without the evidence of parallel versions of more than one passage preserved side by side in the received text, that it has undergone revision at least once, and probably more often. It contains indeed a wide variety of styles, and there is little attempt to fade one into another. The capering verse of the Dromios appears, both openly, and thinly veiled beneath the reviser's prose; sometimes the two are found side by side, as here:

> HOL. O thou monster Ignorance, how deformed doost thou looke.
> NATH. Sir hee hath never fed of the dainties that are bred in a booke.
> He hath not eate paper as it were: He hath not drunke inke.

His intellect is not replenished, hee is onely an animall onely sensible in the duller parts: and such barren plants are set before us, that we thankfull should *be*: which we of taste and feeling are, for those parts that doe fractifie in us more than *he*,

and then back again to jog-verse. In addition to this kind of verse, there are a number of sonnets, and of the *Venus and Adonis* stanza; and the ordinary stuff of the play varies from the tritest of couplets to fine blank verse of the best *Richard II* type. Admirable as the invention is, it is hard to find any poetic method in such a hotch-potch.

*Romeo and Juliet* is a very different matter. This is the first play of Shakspere that can be immediately recognised both as a great poetic, and as a great dramatic whole. The verse is richer and more organic than in the previous plays. The old sing-song "standard" has disappeared; and if there is nothing with quite the poise and control of Richard's great speeches, there is, at the same time, little of the insipid and inadequate verse which marred so much of that play. The most important advance, however, is shown not in the nature, or even in the greater extent of the poetic patches, but in their disposition. Perhaps the plot of this tragedy gives more scope for the legitimate introduction of "cadenzas" than does that of *Richard II*, or of the other plays most closely allied to it; but certain it is that this is the most successful product of Shakspere's first method, the method of what may be called "applied poetry", and as such deserves more detailed examination, both in itself and in the technique by which it is created.

Somewhere I have seen it said that "it is not possible to decorate a structurally efficient play with poetry". The writer of those words should read *Romeo and Juliet*. If a study of the play as it stands does not convince him that Shakspere is here doing exactly what he declares to be impossible, let him turn to the French acting version of Jean Cocteau. In this adaptation all the poetic growths are brutally lopped off, but their roots, the essentially dramatic situations, remain; on the level of purely dramatic effect the play is still a masterpiece, although the clashes of the action no longer strike out the harmonics of poetry. This would be impossible if Shakspere, in the original, had used his poetry to create the action, rather than, as he has done, to emphasise it. The method is in fact that of *Richard II* and of the other plays which we believe him to have written about the middle of the last decade of the sixteenth century. His poetry is still an extraneous device, not an organic part of the plays; with it he will set a scene, cover up a joint in the action, prolong and intensify its climaxes; but it is still possible to strip this poetry off and discover the framework beneath.

The details of this method of "applied poetry", as practised by Shakspere in this play, have already been studied by Mr Granville-Barker in his Preface. I have no wish to repeat what he has set forth so clearly and so completely; in the following notes, therefore, I shall only need to emphasise those points which he, examining the play purely from the producer's point of view, has passed over lightly, points irrelevant to his purpose, though relevant to mine.

There is first a prologue, or argument, cast in sonnet-form, which has much the same effect as a dumb show might have had, in formalising and co-ordinating the whole scheme of the action. The play proper opens with the lively prose of the servants, presenting the first theme of the tragedy, and emphasising admirably all the jarring pettiness of the family feud. This is worked up to the climax of the Duke's sentence, and Shakspere is then ready to introduce the second subject. Romeo, the lover, has taken no part in the brawl, and his entry is carefully prepared by the rather conscious poetry in which his relations discuss him, and which, after the bustle of the first hundred and twenty lines, comes, in Mr Granville-Barker's phrase, "like a change from wood-wind, brass and tympani to an andante on the strings". This cunning modulation at once relaxes the strain and tension of the first movement and creates a soft expectancy for the second, so that Romeo is able to appear as the conventional Elizabethan lover and speak a long succession of devoted couplets.

The next few scenes are chiefly plot-forwarding in purpose, and poetically uninteresting. They are most valuable for the introduction of Old Capulet and Nurse Angelica, to whom I shall return later. The scene following her appearance, that in which Romeo and his companions pass over the stage on their way to the Capulet feast, contains another modulation of importance. The scenes immediately before and after, and the chatter with which this also opens, emphasise the

bustling of the preparations and the more
material side of the gathering. But there is more
in Capulet's reunion than a mere social function;
as the first meeting of the two lovers, it is fateful;
Romeo himself recognises that there is something ominous in the air which attends it. This
partly explains the famous Queen Mab passage,
which must otherwise be set aside as pure
bravura, and the most inexcusable of irrele-
vancies. The scene, as mentioned above, opens
with the light banter of the Maskers; Mercutio's
fairy-tale, which follows quite reasonably upon
what has gone before, alters the tension again,
and infuses just sufficient magic into the atmosphere to make Romeo's sudden foreboding
more worthy of attention, and to prevent it from
jarring on the merriment.

The scene of the gathering itself is as cleverly
managed. The bustle of the servants is continued in the garrulousness of old Capulet,
until the moment when Romeo first catches sight
of Juliet. Then, with his couplets, there falls a
sudden hush. But here Shakspere does not, as
almost any other dramatist would have done,
proceed directly to the meeting of the lovers.
Romeo's musing is interrupted by the bluster of

Tybalt, who argues with Capulet for about forty lines. By the time that he is finally subdued, the lovers have already met—in silence; and now, for their first words to each other, they divide a sonnet between them, thus pressing a powerful seal, as it were, upon their meeting, at once linking themselves together with an invisible bond. But they are not allowed a full love scene yet. The renewed bustle of leave-taking cuts them short; and Shakspere, who has already learnt the value of suspense, a delayed action, and the alternation of scenes, interposes between this and the balcony wooing an act-time, another consolidating sonnet, and Mercutio's high-spirited ribaldries and jests against love. When at last the balcony scene comes, a state of expectancy and receptivity has already been created in the audience.

The expert handling shown in this first section of the play is continued throughout. The method, however, still shows some failings. If *Romeo and Juliet* is compared with Shakspere's later plays, it is seen at once that "applied poetry" is only one dramatic device among many; and when it is used exclusively, as here, its artificiality soon becomes obvious, and it loses much of its effect. This is, of course, most noticeable when two "applications" of poetry are exactly parallel, and it is not always easy to avoid such a repetition. Shakspere has not done so. The return of the Nurse from her errands is twice prepared for in the same way: Juliet soliloquises anxiously and impatiently until the entry of the Nurse, who increases the anxiety, both of her mistress and of the audience, by her complete inability to tell her story straightforwardly. The device of contrast and suspense is highly successful each time, and the soliloquy is an admirable means of isolating Juliet and setting her in an ideal world above the bustle of her relations and guardians; but its repetition calls attention to the artificiality of its lyricism, and through that to the weakness of the whole system. Juliet's cadenzas, though placed with great dramatic effect, are not in themselves dramatic. Compare this:

Gallop apace, you fiery footed steedes,
Towards *Phoebus* lodging, such a Wagoner
As *Phaeton* would whip you to the west,
And bring in Cloudie night immediately.
Spred thy close Curtaine Love-performing night,
That run-awayes eyes may wincke, and *Romeo*
Leape to these armes, untalkt of and unseene,

[ 24 ]

with the words of another anxiously waiting
woman:

That which hath made them drunk, hath made me
    bold:
What hath quench'd them, hath given me fire.
                        Hearke, peace:
It was the owle that shriek'd, the fatal Bell-man,
Which gives the stern'st good-night. He is about it,
    etc.

For all their beauty as poetry, their suitability
to the hour, and the light they throw upon the
speaker's character, I do not feel that Juliet's
lines are organic to the play in the same way as
are Lady Macbeth's, which set a whole scene.
Juliet's soliloquy might be taken out of the play
and spoken as a recitation—though it might not
be very well received by the usual recitation
audience. Lady Macbeth's lines lose point outside their context; they are too much inwoven
with other threads of the play. But *Romeo and
Juliet* is still a dramatic poem, and the poetry
applied poetry, however subtle its application.

Again, Shakspere sometimes attempts, with
the sole aid of this device, effects for which it
is unsuitable or inadequate. There is a pitch of
intensity beyond the range of lyricism, and to

attain it Shakspere seeks to galvanise his poetry into a sort of unnatural vitality by the use of puns and conceits. Examples are Juliet's famous playing upon I—ay—eye,—which I must confess, however, I find not ineffective—and the less successful antitheses of "Beautiful Tyrant, Fiend Angelicall", etc.; worst of all is the strange lamenting of parents, nurse, and bridegroom over the supposed dead body of Juliet:

> NURSE. O wo, O wofull, wofull, wofull day,
> Most lamentable, day, most wofull day,
> That ever, ever, I did yet behold.
> O day, O day, O day, O hatefull day,
> Never was seene so blacke a day as this:
> O wofull day, O wofull day.
> > PARIS. Beguild, divorced, wronged, spighted, slaine, etc.

After all four mourners have had their turn at this, it is not surprising that Friar Laurence should interrupt with "Peace ho! for shame!" The Nurse, in particular, rivals Flute's Thisbe. Something, of course, must be allowed for the fact that the body is only supposedly dead, and the audience know it; the funeral is a mock funeral. But since the Nurse's extravagance, both here and in the scene with Juliet, is partly a burlesque, as Mr Granville-Barker has pointed out, of the speech of the more serious characters, it is presumable that an Elizabethan audience found the latter more or less sincere and convincing. Later Shakspere is to adopt this artificiality as a convention in the representation of certain kinds of emotion; and it would perhaps be better to postpone the whole question, to be dealt with in another place.

So much for the poetic method. Something, too, of the character of the verse has, I hope, appeared in this study of its application; but it may well have been obscured by my insistence on the fact that the poetry of this play is still Poetry, with the one accepted effect of heightening or qualifying emotion, rather than a number of specific kinds of poetry, each with its separate appeal. Actually, though framed for a single use, the verse shows an increased individuality and power of adaptation. The low levels of the action are no longer clothed with perfunctory stuff which has no particular appropriateness; and besides lyrical rhapsodies to cap the peaks, Shakspere has also poetical rhetoric to shape the secondary ridges. Friar Laurence's fine speech to Juliet, as he gives her the potion, has a drive and certainty which forecasts a maturer and more truly dramatic utterance—the Ghost's recital to Hamlet; and even in the stiffer verse of a conventional passage of repartee can be sensed that surety and inevitability that is to reappear in the prose of Hamlet himself:

BENV.  Take thou some new infection to the eye,
And the rank poyson of the old wil die.
ROM.  Your Plantan leafe is excellent for that.
BENV.  For what I pray thee?
ROM.  For your broken skin. etc. etc.

Enter Capulet's servant, and we are almost with Polonius and the Players.

Most important of all, for future developments, is the verse spoken by Juliet's Nurse. The mere fact that she, and perhaps old Capulet too, should speak verse at all, is significant. In an earlier play they would have spoken prose, the buffoon prose that was the recognised medium for the low characters who provided the comic relief. Shakspere had already given a brilliant example of the conventional practice (even supposing that the prose scenes of *Love's Labour's Lost* were later additions) in the prose of Launce. But here he shows his power of reshaping convention: he uses prose to throw a sudden searchlight of realism upon Mercutio at his death, verse to give to the Nurse's speeches that ideal quality, of permanence and inevitability, which only the metrical form can create. In the Nurse's speeches the form is still more or less rigid; read line by line, they may even seem stiff and mechanical, the regular stresses and the pauses at the end of the lines alike insisting that they are decasyllabic blank verse. And yet the first printers, of Quartos good and bad, and of the Folio, set these speeches down as prose. It is possible, of course, that tradition was too strong for them: they knew that the Nurse should have spoken prose, and therefore printed her words as such without question. But it is more likely (especially if these texts derive from a prompt-copy of the play) that the prose-form is due to the fact that these speeches were delivered on the stage as prose, or at least in a colloquial style that contrasted as strongly with the conventional, formalised verse-delivery, as prose would have done.

The Nurse's lines are, in short, an important step in the progress of Shakspere's development of blank verse from the written to the spoken word, from speech-convention to speech.

Shakspere himself was too wise to take the last step of all; his verse always retains the power of idealism beside the power of realism. The true end of the progress is found in Fletcher's experiments, which, by their over-insistent denial of pattern, created a new pattern as rigid as the old. A short quotation will show, I hope, both the formality of the Nurse's speech, and the new absence of constraint:

> *Susan* and she, God rest all Christian soules,
> Were of an age. Well *Susan* is with God,
> She was too good for me.  But as I said,
> On *Lammas* Eve at night shall she be fourteene.
> That shall she marrie, I remember it well.
> 'Tis since the Earth-quake now eleven yeares,
> And she was wean'd I never shall forget it,
> Of all daies of the yeare, upon that day:
> For I had then laid Worme-wood to my Dug
> Sitting in the Sunne under the Dovehouse wall.
> My Lord and you were then at *Mantua*,
> Nay I doe beare a braine.  But as I said,
>                    etc. etc.

I have restored the verse form, to emphasise the strictness of the line-division, though the original punctuation should be emphasis enough in itself.  Compare the almost naïve regularity of the last two lines quoted, with the suppleness of rhythm in the one which precedes them.

*Romeo and Juliet* is, as I have said, the last and greatest of Shakspere's dramatic poems, by which I mean those plays in which the dramatic action is subordinated to the conventions, and ordered (or disordered) by the methods, of non-dramatic poetry. But before leaving this group of plays, there is another, which though not of them is yet akin to them, and should therefore be considered with them. *A Midsummer Night's Dream* is distinguished from the others (except perhaps *Love's Labour's Lost*) by the fact that it was, apparently, not composed for the public theatre, but for performance at a private cele-bration. It is therefore more, perhaps, in the tradition of the masque than of the play proper; yet the methods of its construction are much the same as those of the plays which I have been lately examining. The domination of formal poetry is more marked, as might be expected in a private or court play; rhymed couplets replace standard blank verse in the expositional pas-sages, and the "cadenzas" are more abstract from the dramatic development. The effect of these lyrical flights, in the creation of atmosphere, however, is here more striking than in the other plays. Oberon's description of the wounding of the little western flower, and of the "banke whereon the wilde time blows", help to produce the sense of fairy night in the wood, as Hippolita's hunting reminiscences paint the heroic dawn in the valley; this is that use of poetry for suggestive, almost hypnotic, effect, which is to play such an important part in the mature tragedies, above all in *Macbeth*. But here the poetry overflows the bounds of its application; Shakspere goes on poetising for its own sake, long after the dramatic effect, at which the poetry aimed, is achieved. The poet and the dramatist, in fact, are not yet fused into one.

As a working dramatist Shakspere uses poetry only for the high-lights of his action; and, at the same time, as a poet he is too highly conscious of himself and his poetic duty, so that he is capable of putting into the mouth of Hermia, under the disguise of poetry, this trite and quite superfluous lecture upon the physical effects of darkness:

> Dark night, that from the eye his function takes,
> The eare more quicke of apprehension makes
> Wherein it doth impaire the seeing sense,
> It paies the hearing double recompence.

[ 32 ]

Thou art not by mine eye, *Lysander*, found,
Mine eare (I thanke it) brought me to that sound.

If this play had been intended (as, we are told, it
was not) for representation before an uncultured
audience in an open-air theatre, where the pre-
sence of night required constant references in the
text to make it plain, there would have been some
excuse for this, though not for its elaboration;
in an indoor production, however lyrical, it is
even less excusable. Shakspere had not yet
learned economy; and that learning is now to be
studied.

# PART II

## THE TRANSITION

**M**OST of the plays hitherto examined have belonged to the category of dramatic poems, or poeticised drama; those which Shakspere was to write later in life are true poetic drama, and their material is dramatic poetry. It is possible to perform a good deal of hocus-pocus and epigrammatical jugglery with these terms, but the distinction remains clear. In the earlier plays the poetry is often indulged at the expense of a properly proportioned dramatic structure; or at least the two interests, poetry and drama, are kept separate, and independent of each other. In the later, the one cannot be divided from the other; they have become a single instrument.

This fusion is partly due to a new co-ordinating impulse, which came to govern Shakspere's work about the middle of the last decade of the sixteenth century. *King John* and *The Merchant of Venice* are, compared with what has gone before, very level plays. The old tricks and devices still abound. There are plenty of couplets, and even the slipshod, delayed rhymes, noticed in his first historical plays, recur frequently; Kydian turns are common, and series of lines that end with the same word, as the famous "ring" passage in the last scene of the *Merchant*, and Constance's successive plays on "fears", "content", and "need" in *John III* (i); quatrains, too, and stanzas still appear embedded in the blank verse. But all these are now more organic to the play. The couplets are no longer haphazard, but make a point or conclude an argument; the turns are decorations which show off the artificiality of such deliberately conventional scenes as those of repartee or lament; the Bastard's rhymes are intended as gibes at affected propriety and politeness, and Bassanio's quatrain is a lyrical rounding-off of the fundamentally unrealistic casket scene.

The co-ordinating impulse which has toned these patches into the fabric of the play, and at the same time made that very fabric itself more cohesive, more a living growth, is Shakspere's newly acquired command of rhetorical construction; of all those powers noticed in the great speeches of *Richard II*, which were, I believe, added to the original play, or elaborated upon its foundation, at this time. In these plays,

and in those which immediately follow, Shakspere is experimenting with rhetoric to produce a
more concentrated energy in the development of
his action than was possible in a mainly lyrical
drama. The poetry is there still; but it is a
natural and essential growth of the speaker's
emotion or argument (in these plays generally
the latter). So that even so striking a line as the
famous "singing Masons building roofes of
Gold" does not seem extravagant in its surroundings—and indeed the Salic Law, and
Henry's foreign policy, are surroundings sober
enough in all conscience; but the simile appears
as a rhetorical ornament, almost as a picturesque
gesture of the speaker, or the flashing of the
Archbishop's jewelled ring as he raises his hand
to emphasise his point.

But merely to increase the wavelength, though
it may give more force and drive to each individual wave, does not destroy the regularity of
the progression. These cumulative periods and
soaring flights can sustain and carry forward a
scene as the earlier, more closely patterned, verse
could not; but their monotony is, if anything,
even more oppressive. The reader soon tires of
a state where every councillor is a Cicero, and the

long-winded vaunts and reminiscences of the Welsh Wizard are the rule rather than the exception among the reputed men of action. The verse of these plays, in short, for all its general brilliance of construction, is often not far removed from such terrible argumentative megaphoning as was later produced by its imitators. Shakspere was saved, however, from degenerating into an earlier Massinger by the vigour and energy with which he was at the same time elaborating another branch of his craft, the prose speech.

I have already said something of Elizabethan convention in the use of prose, and Shakspere's adaptation of it. So long as prose was essentially a comic medium, and low comic at that, it was impossible that it should attain any great height of dramatic expression. Shakspere had exploited it to the full in the admirably written fooling of Launce, the butts of *Love's Labour's Lost*, and the rude mechanicals of *A Midsummer Night's Dream*; but he had also extended its capabilities, in giving prose to Mercutio, not only in moments of light-heartedness, as to several of his predecessors, but for his dying speech. The next great landmark in the development of prose is

*The Merchant of Venice.* The Gobbos worthily uphold the old tradition: new potentialities are revealed in Shylock's great speech in vindication of the Jews:

> ...he hath disgrac'd me, and hindered me halfe a million, laught at my losses, mockt at my gaines, scorned my Nation, thwarted my bargaines, cooled my friends, heated my enemies, and what's the reason? I am a *Jewe*: Hath not a *Jew* eyes? hath not a *Jew* hands, organs, dementions, sences, affections, passions, fed with the same foode, hurt with the same weapons, subject to the same diseases, healed by the same meanes, warmed and cooled by the same Winter and Sommer as a Christian is: if you pricke us do we not bleede? if you tickle us, doe we not laugh? if you poison us, doe we not die? and if you wrong us, shall we not revenge? if we are like you in the rest, we will resemble you in that. If a *Jew* wrong a *Christian*, what is his humility? revenge. If a *Christian* wrong a *Jew*, what should his sufferance be by Christian example? why revenge. The villanie you teach me I will execute, and it shall goe hard but I will better the instruction.

This prose is more highly wrought than any which has gone before, and it has a concentration of which Shakspere's verse at that date was quite incapable. The vicious, hurdling movement of the first phrases; the point of rest, the node, "I am a *Jewe*"; the chanting intensity of the parallel clauses which follow, becoming ever more exalted and prophetic towards the end of the speech: none of these effects, much less their combination, was possible in a blank verse as long-limbed and ungainly as was Shakspere's then. Even the more obvious devices, such as the damnable iteration of the key-phrases "revenge", and, in the preceding speech, "Let him looke to his bond", need, for their full effect, a closer texture in the surrounding and supporting fabric.

There is another quality appearing first in prose and later worked out in verse, which is harder to define. It is found most strikingly in Hamlet's great prose speeches, but may here be illustrated from Falstaff:

BARD. Why, Sir *John*, my Face does you no harme.
FALST. No, Ile be sworne: I make as good use of it, as many a man doth of a Deaths-Head, or a *Memento Mori*. I never see thy Face, but I thinke upon Hell fire, and *Dives* that lived in Purple; for there he is in his Robes burning, burning.

or in the Second Part:

Men of all sorts take a pride to gird at mee; the braine of this foolish compounded clay, Man, is not able to invent any thing that tends to laughter, more than I invent, or is invented on me.

Falstaff has a trick of voice that recalls the great prose writers of the seventeenth century, the doctors and divines. He shows here the same curious combination of abandon and economy, the fine frenzy blended with and wrought into an inevitable rhythmic movement, that is so characteristic of their work. His words have the air of being spoken extempore, and yet being under the strictest control; and so, by some sort of equal and opposite tension, acquire a new momentum.

Controlled energy is indeed the natural end of all these tendencies in Shakspere's development. The rhetorical experiment had made the poetry organic to the action and to the speaker, so that he was now able to take it in his stride, instead of pausing and, with folded hands, launching into the lyrical flight. The cultivation of prose had shown the possibility of a new vigour, dependent on restraint, and manifested both in a more powerful and various rhythm which might break up the measured regularity of the verse, and also in a new forcefulness of language. And these are chief among the qualities of Shakspere's mature verse.

# PART III

## DRAMATIC POETRY

### §1. THE STAPLE VERSE

THE danger of attempting to group Shakspere's works under definite phases has been already emphasised; I need only add that such terms as "mature plays" and "final style" are among the most misleading of all. Shakspere, having avoided the slough of rhetoric, never allowed himself to rest, or his method to stagnate. Throughout the "period" of the great tragedies he is still experimenting, still searching after a type of verse that would give his thought at once greater concentration and greater freedom. This search had two branches: experiments with language, and experiments with rhythms and what may be called "tone". A rough distinction may be made, that in the earlier tragedies Shakspere was most occupied with language, in the late with rhythm and tone. But the two are, of course, very much interwoven; development of the one meant development of the other, so that minor adjustments were constantly being made to both throughout the period. The whole process is best studied in detailed analysis and comparison of representative speeches chosen from the whole series of plays following *Julius Caesar*. This I propose to do; but must first say something of the larger rhythm of the plays, of the connection between successive speeches, in short of the dialogue-framework in which they are units.

Dialogue, as such, was less essential to Elizabethan drama than it is to most modern plays. There were, of course, the flytings and contests of wit; there were also, in the early plays, those decorative patterns of which the stichomuthia of Richard and Elizabeth, or the alternating laments of the dirge over Juliet, are obvious examples already quoted. These passages are, however, static in their effect; that is, they may define various emotions in the speaker and arouse them in the audience, but they cause no spiritual development or revolution in either. The true dramatic crises, the dynamic effects which do achieve this, are found in single speeches. For, the feelings of an Elizabethan drama being always explicit, always elaborated in the text, it was possible to sum up fully and clearly, in the

[ 42 ]

reaction of a single character, a situation and its emotional consequences which to-day would have to be deduced from the interaction of half a dozen speeches.

Dialogue, then, in the modern sense, was only used (apart from the decorative effects already noticed) for contrast, and for preparation. The device at its crudest can be seen in the second scene of *The Tempest*: Miranda's lack of attention, and her attempts to disguise it with such over-acted protestations as "Your tale, Sir, would cure deafnesse", are only necessary in order to diversify the smooth eloquence of Prospero's rich and fruity baritone, which would otherwise be tedious beyond endurance. From this derives the obvious use of rapid dialogue to quicken up a scene, to create a sense of excitement, of tension. When Macbeth returns from murdering Duncan, the "horrid expectancy" of his scene with Lady Macbeth is due primarily to that first breathless interchange:

LADY. Did not you speake?
MACB.      When?
LADY.            Now.
MACB.                  As I descended?
LADY. I.            etc. etc.

And Hamlet's agitation at hearing of the appearance of his father's ghost is apparent in the rapid questions which he puts to the witnesses and their equally hurried answers. More elaborate examples of the same use of dialogue are that conversation with Iago which first stirs Othello's jealousy, where the natural effect of question and reply is reinforced by that use of repeated phrases already noticed in Shylock's great speech—a favourite device in this play, for besides Iago's "Honest" and "Thinke, my Lord?" there are the famous demands for the handkerchief, and Emilia's "My husband? My husband say that she was false?"; and the last scene of the second act of *Lear*, where it is again associated with repetition. This last is on a much larger scale. Many of the individual utterances have been extended into continuous speeches that are complete and dramatic in themselves. But the principle is the same: Lear's persistent questions flog the emotion ever to a greater agony of intensity: "Who put my man i' th' stockes? Who stockt my servant? How came my man i' th' Stockes?" and later "Returne with her?" three times repeated. As the scene proceeds, the buzzing questions of Regan and Gonerill, on either side

[ 44 ]

of Lear, make the tension almost unbearable: "What fifty Followers? What should you need...? Why might not you...? Why not, my Lord? What need you five and twenty? What need one?" And upon that comes the dynamic speech, "O reason not the need", and Lear's tempestuous exit.

Each separate unit in this progression and interaction of speeches is too extended, too elaborate, too dramatic in itself, for the whole to be considered merely as a straightforward piece of dialogue. But even this sequence—and here is the point I want to make—like the less heavily charged sequences of *Macbeth*, *Hamlet*, and *Othello*, is incomplete in itself. It is summed up and resolved in the storm, just as Macbeth's rapid interchange is resolved in the hysterical rapture of the "sleep" passage, Hamlet's in the musing which ends the scene, Othello's in the "curse of marriage" soliloquy. These longer speeches are at once the climax and epitome of the dramatic processes; in them the feeling of a whole progression is focussed, and the method of its working-out reproduced in little. It is therefore in these crises of the action that Shakspere's exploitation of poetry for dramatic ends can most

easily be studied in detail; and the passages chosen
for analysis here are as nearly as possible all of
this type. As a link with what has gone before,
I should like to take first a speech from *Julius
Caesar*, which still retains something of the
rhetorical tang of the great chronicle plays. The
phrasing is governed largely by the orator's
tricks of the deferred climax and the illuminating
afterthought; the images either flash out with
the orator's aptness, or are developed at his easy
and elegant length. The self-confidence, the un-
hurried surety of the whole effect, all are the
orator's. Some of these qualities can be seen in
Brutus' great soliloquy:

It must be by his death: and for my part,
I know no personall cause, to spurne at him,
But for the generall. He would be crown'd:
How that might change his nature, there's the
      question?
It is the bright day, that brings forth the Adder,
And that craves warie walking: Crowne him that,
And then I graunt we put a Sting in him
That at his will he may doe danger with.
Th' abuse of Greatnesse, is, when it dis-joynes
Remorse from Power: And to speake truth of *Caesar*,
I have not knowne, when his Affections sway'd
More then his Reason. But 'tis a common proofe,

[ 46 ]

That Lowlynesse is young Ambition's Ladder,
Whereto the Climber upward turnes his Face:
But when he once attaines the upmost Round,
He then unto the Ladder turnes his Backe,
Lookes in the Clouds, scorning the base degrees
By which he did ascend: so *Caesar* may:
Then least he may, prevent. And since the Quarrell
Will beare no colour, for the thing he is.
Fashion is thus; that what he is, augmented,
Would run to these, and these extremities:
And therefore thinke him as a Serpents egge,
Which hatch'd, would as his kinde grow mischievous;
And kill him in the shell.

The fact that Brutus is a philosopher will not alone account for the philosophical air which hangs over this speech, for every other speaker in the play is as much inspired by it as Brutus; an air that manifests itself not only in the judicious citation of saws and "common proofes", but also in the extraordinary orderliness of the whole. The themes are concisely and tonelessly stated: "It must be by his death", "He would be crown'd"; and from them springs the leisurely, but beautifully coherent and organic growth of armchair reasoning. It is so competently done, yet so coldly calculating; there is no pulse of emotion behind it. The lengths of the sentences are exquisitely varied, but not their paces; and though such graceful elaborations as the adder-image, which drags its slow length along through the succeeding sentences, or the equally lingering ladder, carry the mind forward from the main themes in a pleasant muse, there is no sense, at the end of it all, of a progress made or an objective gained. Even the intonation is self-conscious. The speaker is always listening to the modulations of his own voice; and it is easy to see the studied movement of the hand which must accompany such a phrase as "these, and these extremities". Worst of all is the Dramatic (by which I mean melodramatic) effect of those significant and lip-smacking pauses: "so *Caesar* may: then least he may, prevent", and "thinke him as a Serpents egge...; and kill him in the shell".

Compare with this a speech of Hamlet:

Now might I do it pat, now he is praying,
And now Ile doo't, and so he goes to Heaven,
And so am I reveng'd: that would be scann'd,
A Villaine kills my Father, and for that
I his soule Sonne, do this same Villaine send
To heaven. Oh this is hyre and Sallery, not Revenge.
He tooke my Father grossely, full of bread,

[ 48 ]

With all his Crimes broad blowne, as fresh as May.
And how his Audit stands, who knowes, save Heaven;
But in our circumstance and course of thought
'Tis heavie with him; and am I then reveng'd,
To take him in the purging of his Soule,
When he is fit and season'd for his passage? No.
Up Sword, and know thou a more horrid hent
When he is drunke asleepe: or in his Rage,
Or in th' incestuous pleasure of his bed,
At gaming, swearing, or about some acte
That has no rellish of Salvation in't,
Then trip him, that his heeles may kicke at Heaven,
And that his Soule may be as damn'd and blacke
As Hell, whereto it goes.

Modern editions have done their best to order
this speech as Brutus' speech is ordered; but the
essential difference in the movement remains
obvious in spite of all that heavy stopping can
do towards "tying leaden pounds to 's heeles".
The verse of *Julius Caesar*, at best, glibly per-
suades the hearer to feel an emotion; if this does
not at once rush him into feeling, it has not
achieved its aim. The secret of its effect is the
constant change of pace. The speech opens with
an even muttering; on "that would be scann'd"
the voice rises and broadens—to be stifled by the
full-stop of modern editors, who take "scanned"

merely as a synonym for "adversely criticised".
But if the punctuation of the early texts is followed, and "scanned" taken as meaning "inter-
preted" as well as "criticised" (the interpre-
tation being the next line and a half), the whole
becomes a single crescendo and accelerando to
"heaven". And here Shakspere uses one of his
favourite devices: the momentary checking of
the wave in the very second of its breaking. On
"heaven" the whole force of the progression
hangs poised and quivering in the air; the crash
comes with "Oh this is hyre and Sallery".
Exactly similar is the "No!" which ends a later
sequence of this same speech. Both these climax-
phrases are printed by the second Quarto (and
modern editions) in a separate line. This emphasises the pause before the thunder, and its
thunderousness when it comes, but may obscure
the fact (so obvious in the froth and flurry of the
Folio's jumbled line) that it is very much a part
of the gathering wave that prepares for it.

After the first crisis, the speech starts again at a
lower level. The change of voice can be felt, with
its attempt at reasoning restraint which soon
gives way to the wailing cadences of "with all
his Crimes broad blowne, as fresh as May", etc.

These, in their turn, fade into a heavy sigh of pity and doubt, weighed down with the reflective doublet of nouns, "our circumstance and course of thought"; and thence springs the second rapid crescendo, culminating in the "No!" already referred to, and followed immediately by another— not a simple progression this time, but one of those leap-frog movements (Shakspere is very fond of them) in which the first flight is checked before the climax is reached, and its successor starts again at a lower pitch, to go beyond it, thus:

> Up Sword, and know thou a more horrid hent
> When he is drunke asleepe:
> > or in his Rage, or in  etc. etc.

The double wave finally topples over in the triumphant phrase "then trip him", and what follows is only the extension and elaboration of this triumph.

The foregoing analysis may have been too detailed to be easily followed, or, if followed, to be accepted in full. The only point, however, on which I insist, is the importance of pace and tone-variations in the general effect, showing a marked advance in technical resource over the rather staid and text-book methods of *Julius Caesar*.

This particular speech of Hamlet is admittedly something of a prodigy in its surroundings. The play as a whole is more striking for its development of language than for its exploitation of rhythm; that development was, in fact, at a stage which did not make for rhythmical flexibility, but rather opposed it.

In studying *Richard II* I have already mentoned Shakspere's gradual rejection of the laboured simile for the swift metaphor, and the plain metaphor in favour of a shifting of mixed kind. *Julius Caesar* contains the full-length simile or metaphor (though its elaboration is more tactful than in the earlier plays) side by side with the sudden luminous image, which lights up the speech while remaining an organic part of it:

Conceptions onely proper to myselfe,
Which give some Soyle (perhaps) to my behaviours.

*Hamlet* represents the second stage of this progress, which is to end in the complete freedom and flexibility of Antony's:

> The hearts
> That spannielled me at heeles, to whom I gave
> Their wishes, do dis-Candie, melt their sweets
> On blossoming *Caesar*: And this Pine is barkt
> That over-top'd them all.

The verse of *Hamlet* is already packed with shifting metaphors throughout; but the favourite device for procuring the shift is the rather conscious one of the doublet, of replacing a single adjective by two having slightly different meanings, so that the sense quivers and blurs even as it is apprehended. Such phrases as "extravagant and erring spirit", "ponderous and marble jawes", "turbulent and dangerous lunacies", carry an overtone of meaning; more meaning is concentrated in them than lies in the plain sense of the words, for the two slightly discordant adjectives suggest a third, a blend of the two, which is, in fact, non-existent. An even more effective variant of the device is the phrase containing a pair of qualifying nouns—"the pales and forts of reason", "the teeth and forehead of our faults". Here, as the images are more defined in their diversity, so the effect of yoking them together is more striking.

Shakspere had, of course, used both these tricks many times before the writing of *Hamlet*; and they are common enough outside Shakspere, particularly among the more philosophical authors, as, for instance (*absit omen*) Bacon in his ornamental mood. But nowhere are doublets more persistently employed than in *Hamlet*. The effect of this is to slow up the verse, and to give it a curiously reflective cast. The ambiguity of the doublet certainly introduces a new wealth of meaning, but its circuitousness tends to make the line ponderous and unwieldy. In the plays which follow, the problem-comedies and *Othello*, Shakspere learns to use the device less monotonously, and to combine it with the new rhythmical vitality. An early example of this combination is the speech of Hamlet already quoted; another is Isabella's plea, in *Measure for Measure*:

> Mercifull heaven,
> Thou rather with thy sharpe and sulpherous bolt
> Splits the un-wedgable and gnarled Oke,
> Then the soft Mertill: But man, proud man,
> Drest in a little briefe authoritie,
> Most ignorant of what he's most assur'd,
> (His glassie Essence) like an angry Ape
> Plaies such phantastique tricks before high heaven,
> As makes the Angels weepe:

where, after the gnashing and champing of the opening, the speaker takes a deep breath and starts away to a more direct climax.

*Troilus and Cressida* and *Othello* both contain special uses of verse which must be considered in a later section. But for the most part, the plays of this date consolidate and exploit the position won, without attempting any new advance in technique. It is another period of rest, of level competence comparable to that of the rhetorical plays. In *King Lear* the signs of another change are already apparent. The speeches of Lear himself are again a special subject; it is in those of the other main characters, particularly the "bad people", that a new method can be sensed—or rather a lack of method, for it is the uncertainty of this verse, its total loss of spontaneity and inevitability, which casts that ghostly shade of uneasiness over many an early reading of *King Lear*. At first this may be put down to the verse being stilted, the fit reflection of the formal and ungenerous characters of its speakers. But closer examination shows that it is nothing of the sort; its awkwardness comes not from its formality but from its unformed colloquialism. Shakspere is making a further move away from the "paper of verses" and towards the recording of the speaking voice.

Some of the courtliness of verse, the artificiality of line-division, had been already destroyed when, in *Hamlet*, Shakspere had written speeches obviously intended for an emotional

delivery which would ultimately be more powerful in shaping the speech than the verse-form. In
*King Lear* he carries the process a step further;
the emotionalism, if I may call it that, the shaping
impulse of feeling, is there even before the speech
comes to be delivered, for the verse-form itself
has been shaken up into something vital and
personal to the speech. The sense of awkwardness, in *King Lear*, is due to the conscious
thoroughness with which this shaking up is done.
This is Shakspere's nearest approach to the
spirit, if not to the practice, of Fletcher. Compare a speech of Edmund with an Othello parallel.
This is how Iago plots:

And what's he then, that saies I play the villaine?
When this advice is free I give, and honest,
Proball to thinking, and indeed the course
To win the Moore again. For 'tis most easie
Th' inclyning *Desdemona* to subdue
In any honest Suite. She's fram'd as fruitefull
As the free Elements. And then for her
To win the Moore, were't to renownce his Baptisme,
All seales, and Simbols of redeemed sin:
His Soule is so enfetter'd to her Love,
That she may make, unmake, do what she list,
Even as her Appetite shall play the God,
With his weake Function.

And here is Edmund:

To both these Sisters have I sworne my love:
Each jealous of the other, as the stung
Are of the Adder. Which of them shall I take?
Both? One? Or neither? Neither can be enjoy'd
If both remaine alive: To take the Widdow,
Exasperates, makes mad her Sister *Gonerill*,
And hardly shall I carry out my side,
Her husband being alive. Now then, wee'l use
His countenance for the Battaile, which being done,
Let her who would be rid of him, devise
His speedy taking off.

Both these speeches rely for much of their effect
on the impromptu succession of the thoughts,
not in any particularly logical order, which crop
up one after the other, each with its pause and
accompanying change of intonation. It is this
which gives to each, in actual performance, its
variety—and they are cleverly varied. And yet
it would be possible to read Iago's lines with
an even declamation that is unthinkable for
Edmund's. Iago's lines have a deliberate sonority and measure which has been as deliberately
bounced out of Edmund's by the inclusion of
such easygoing phrases as "Which of them shall
I take?" or that unashamedly lolloping line,
"(wee'l use) His countenance for the Battaile,

which being done, etc." The solemn doublets have disappeared; or, at least, "exasperates, makes mad" is but a hobbledehoyish substitute for the "rend and deracinate" of former days (there is unfortunately no example in Edmund's speech of the clumsy compounds, "not-to-be-endured riots", "death-practis'd Duke", etc., etc., which seem to me to be the more legitimate heirs of the doublet's position). Finally, to come down to pure metrics, the same looseness is revealed, not only in the increased number of feminine endings, but also in that fondness (an equally Fletcherian characteristic) for the weak caesura followed by a jumble of resolved feet, which gives to the line that curious air of being ungirt about the middle. Gonerill provides a better example than Edmund:

> I...now grow fearefull...
> That you protect this course, and put it on
> By your allowance, which if you should, the fault
> Would not scape censure, nor the redresses sleepe,
> etc. etc.

All these changes are rebellions against the line. Not that line-division was thereby to be completely smothered into oblivion; on the contrary, much of the force and freedom of these variations is due to the tacit acknowledgment of the decasyllabic, end-stopped norm behind them, as in this speech from *Macbeth*:

If it were done, when 'tis done, then 'twer well,
It were done quickly: If th' Assassination
Could trammell up the Consequence, and catch
With his surcease, Successe: that but this blow
Might be the be all, and the end all. Heere,
But heere, upon this Banke and Schoole of time,
Wee'ld jumpe the life to come. But in these Cases,
We still have judgement heere, that we but teach
Bloody Instructions, which being taught, returne
To plague th' Inventer. This even-handed Justice
Commends th' Ingredience of our poyson'd Challice
To our owne lips.

The first half of this speech recalls the *Hamlet* passage quoted above. There is the same muttered opening, followed by the same rapid crescendo (this time a double one, the leap-frog type) with the same pause at the summit of the wave before the crash comes. But in Hamlet's speech the crash was not allowed to interfere with the line-scheme—either carefully isolated from the rest, *extra metrum*, or bundled together with it into a nondescript line where it could do no harm. Macbeth's "Heere, but heere...", on the other hand, is an integral part of the metre, and its force disrupts and shatters the whole framework; it is "the most powerful effect possible in a blank verse line".

In the second part of the speech can be seen the mellowing of *King Lear's* raw colloquialism. The feminine ending, the weak caesura, and the resolved foot are still there, but, in spite of their unsettling influence, the lines have acquired a new sonority and a new cohesion, very different from the suave progressions of *Hamlet* or *Othello*, and yet, in their own way, quite as impressive, with the added freedom and forcefulness of irregularity. This, however, is perhaps not a fair example; for *Macbeth*, with its peculiar circumstances, is something of a freak. It is the verse of *Antony and Cleopatra* which is the best comment on that of Lear:

Yes like enough: hye-battel'd *Caesar* will
Unstate his happinesse, and be Stag'd to th' shew
Against a Sworder. I see mens Judgements are
A parcell of their Fortunes, and things outward
Do draw the inward quality after them
To suffer all alike, that he should dreame,
Knowing all measures, the full *Caesar* will
Answer his emptinesse; *Caesar* thou hast subdu'd
His judgement too.

Enobarbus' speech has more body than Edmund's, more directness and economy than Gonerill's. All the awkward elements are there, even the double-barrelled adjective; but they have been wrought into a verse-fabric where the full-length "sentiment" and the more vivid pattern of pace and tone-variations can exist side by side in perfect harmony. Even Hamlet's change from the frenzy of

He tooke my Father grossely, full of bread,
With all his Crimes broad blowne, as fresh as May,
And how his Audit stands, who knowes, save Heaven;

to the reflective

But in our circumstance and course of thought
'Tis heavie with him;

seems abrupt and unskilled beside Enobarbus' subtle modulation from cold and impersonal moralising to the warm, practical indignation of "that he should dreame—". Nor must it be supposed, because the transition is so easy, that this verse is only the boiling down of extremes into a robust and all-containing homogeneity, and that as such it cannot rise or fall to the more striking effects. It can be swift as well

as staid, exuberant as well as restrained: witness
Antony's
                                Mine Nightingale,
We have beate them to their Beds. What Gyrle,
      though gray
Do something mingle with our yonger brown, yet
      ha' we
A Braine that nourishes our Nerves, and can
Get gole for gole of youth.

The point is not that the verse is incapable of
variation, but that in all its varieties, wrought
reflection or fine frenzy, is present that sense
of control which yoked the abandon and the
economy of Falstaff's words, and made such a
forceful instrument of Shakspere's prose. In
*Antony and Cleopatra* the full translation of the
great prose qualities into verse is accomplished.

"Last scene of all...is second childishness";
Jaques' dictum, if it be not taken in too dero-
gatory a sense, is applicable to Shakspere's
technique of dramatic verse. For in his last plays,
the second part of *Pericles*, *Cymbeline*, *Winter's
Tale*, and *Tempest*, he makes something of a·
return to his old practice. Rhetoric and the
lyrical cadenza reappear; in addition, the connection of scenes and situations is slackened, and
the characters become more stiff and allegorical;

[ 62 ]

indeed the division, so strikingly marked in these plays, between wicked age and innocent youth, approaches the ideal distinction of Blake's *Innocence* and *Experience*, and the character types are as formal as those of age. Many reasons have been suggested for this sudden change. Most probable it is that Shakspere, who had before shown himself something of a time-server, was again complying with the desires of his public. While Marlowe and Greene were still in vogue he had written "tragicall histories" and more or less pastoral comedies; when Heywood set the fashion, Shakspere followed him with romanticised chronicles containing a low-life or citizen plot; a crop of comedies all turning on disguise answered the craze for disguises which had been fostered by Chapman in such fantastical quick-change plays as the *Blind Beggar of Alexandria*; *Measure for Measure* was in tune with Middleton's slick realism, and *Hamlet* followed Marston's revival of the revenge play. Finally *Cymbeline* appears in close company with *Philaster*. The change of type was so sweeping, that it demanded a change of method, and Shakspere now returned to the old devices, which found here a new appropriateness.

Those who possess a vivid mental picture of Shakspere's old age have suggested a further explanation; he had grown bored, they say, was no longer trying, had ceased really to care about the writing of plays. To me Shakspere's interest in playwriting seems rather to have quickened, but to have turned more to the technical side of composition, to the mechanical contriving of situations as situations, and to the writing of poetry as poetry. He is no longer concerned primarily with the building up of an action in the Aristotelian sense, in the emotions arising from the interrelation of characters, or indeed in the interrelation itself, except in so far as it presents a problem in manipulation. Thus Shakspere's last plays are a strange mixture of involved situations, cleverly and painstakingly worked out, and purely lyrical scenes, which appear to exist only for the purpose of providing an opportunity for poetry unfettered by dramatic needs. The characters are now either black and white pawns, to be moved into ingenious positions and counter-positions, or appropriately painted mouth-pieces for the speaking of non-dramatic verse.

Thus the first two acts of *Cymbeline* compose an intrigue plot which is worked out with the greatest care and success. The scene in which Iachimo first sounds Imogen may rank with the most subtly written in all the tragedies. But it is only in the machinery of the situations that Shakspere is really interested; where a short cut is possible, he takes it. In an earlier play Posthumus' reaction to Iachimo's apparent success— "Is there no way for men to be, but women Must be halfe-workers?"—would not, I feel, have been crammed up in a single soliloquy, magnificently wrought poetry as it is. The intrigue successfully carried out, Shakspere loses interest in the dramatic side of the play, and turns to a romantic Wales. Only at the end he takes up all the threads again, and writes a dramatic resolution, which, in its mechanical cleverness and excessive neatness, might almost be a deliberate caricature of the stage *dénouement*.

In the same way, the first part of *The Winter's Tale* is a complete tragic plot in miniature. At an earlier stage Shakspere might have devoted a whole play to this story of the husband whose unfounded jealousy destroys both his wife and children; but now the whole plot, compressed, but still perfect in every part, only occupies three acts in the telling. The abruptness of the effect

can be partly explained by the fact that Shakspere
has here, as in *Cymbeline*, disentangled the sub-
plot from the main and tacked it on at the end,
thus robbing the main action of that stereoscopic
quality, that standing out from a background,
which the simultaneous development of the sub-
plot would have given it. But that the plot of the
first three acts is one stripped to its essentials is
everywhere apparent. Leontes falls in and out
of jealousy with wonderful suddenness, for
emotional processes are no longer of first importance to Shakspere. It is only the facts of
jealousy and repentance that he needs for the
framework of his plot. And again, the plot con-
cluded, he retires to a maritime Bohemia to
indulge his poetry in a sort of pastoral, or masque
of shepherds; an exaltation of pure poetry which
*The Tempest* repeats in the person of Prospero,
who stands apart from the dramatic action, producing poetry and conjuring tricks in a single
breath.

Under these new conditions, the verse falls
into two classes; the poetry of the pastoral scenes
is naturally very different from that needed for
scenes of compressed action. The taut, spare
action-plots of the later plays demand a verse of

extraordinary compactness and concentration—
the verse of *Antony and Cleopatra* made even more
flexible, even more capable of presenting, as a
natural sequence, the sudden shifts in the thought,
the hints and ironies which, in the development
of the action, have taken the place of detailed
explanation and elaboration of feeling. This
greater flexibility is obtained partly by introducing more resolved feet and even further dis-
regarding the line-unit, partly by more frequent
and unprepared changes in tone, which are most
commonly engineered by means of the paren-
thesis.

Shakspere had, of course, used parentheses for
this purpose very much earlier than in *Cymbeline*
—both the single apologetic or explanatory
word:

some Soyle (perhaps) for my behaviours,

and the longer, more deliberately inconsequential
phrase:

Admit no other way to save his life
(As I subscribe not that, nor any other,
But in the losse of question) that you, his Sister
etc. etc.

[ 67 ]

But it is in *Cymbeline*, where a single packed speech so often replaces pages of dialogue in earlier plays, that this device becomes indispensable, as providing a substitute tone-variation for that between two separate speakers; and its great effectiveness for pointing an irony—such a common weapon in these late plays—is additional excuse for Shakspere's abundant use of it in the verse of the intrigue scenes. Of this Cymbeline's Queen will provide a good example:

> I wonder, Doctor,
> Thou ask'st me such a Question: Have I not bene
> Thy Pupill long? Hast thou not learn'd me how
> To make Perfumes? Distill? Preserve? Yea so,
> That our great King himselfe doth woo me oft
> For my Confections? Having thus far proceeded,
> (Unlesse thou think'st me divellish) is't not meete
> That I did amplifie my judgement in
> Other Conclusions? I will try the forces
> Of these thy Compounds, on such Creatures as
> We count not worth the hanging (but none humane)
> To try the vigour of them, and apply
> Allayments to their Act, and by them gather
> Their severall vertues, and effects.

This is a very smooth speech. There are no changes of pace, no striking pauses, no great "effects" of any kind. The Queen is one of those royal mothers, common to fairy-tale traditions and the Elizabethan drama from Tamora to Brunhalt, whose cunning is only equalled by their cruelty; and her speech is therefore as restrained as befits a female Machiavel. Nevertheless an extraordinary flexibility, it might almost be said sinuosity, is given to it by the easy conversationalism of the rhythm, and the changes of tone of which the parentheses provide the chief. Furthermore these parentheses supply, by implication, the two most important points in the speech: "(unlesse thou think'st me divellish)" tells us, the audience, that we, at least, should be very sure that she is so: "(none humane)" hints that it is precisely upon human beings that the Queen will make her experiments.

Parentheses appear even more thickly in *The Winter's Tale*, especially in the part of Leontes, whose disjointed mutterings they admirably portray; and in *The Tempest* there is a riot of them, which often holds up an argument or narrative for lines together:

Although this Lord of weake remembrance; this
Who shall be of as little memory
When he is earth'd, hath here almost persuaded
(For hee's a Spirit of persuasion, onely

[ 69 ]

Professes to persuade) the King his sonne's alive
'Tis as impossible that hee's undrown'd,
As he that sleepes heere, swims.

In this, the first office of the parentheses is to point the jokes, as the pun between remembrance and memory. But the clogged and labouring motion of the opening makes the climax of the last two lines all the more swift and direct, thus producing the appearance of a change of pace where in fact none is; or, to put it another way, Shakspere has made the change inherent in the plain sound of the verse, without relying upon the actor's delivery to bring it out.

Compare this with Isabella's plea, quoted earlier, where the change is left much more to the actor; Isabella is carefully invited to help the speech to its climax, whereas Antonio's lines will make their effect however he chooses to deliver them.

The verse of the pastoral characters is altogether smoother and simpler. It is in many ways a return to an earlier type. Resolutions, abbreviations, and inversions are fewer; the pleasantly fluent lines are again for the most part true decasyllables, with an occasional easy lapping over into the feminine ending; and the mythology even, and extravagant imagery, of the *Venus and Adonis* period reappears:

> Apprehend
> Nothing but jollity: the Goddes themselves
> (Humbling their Deities to love) have taken
> The shapes of Beasts upon them. Jupiter
> Became a Bull, and bellow'd: the greene Neptune
> A Ram, and bleated: and the Fire-roab'd God
> Golden Apollo, a poore humble Swaine,
> As I seeme now. Their transformations,
> Were never for a peece of beauty rarer,
> Nor in a way so chaste: since my desires
> Run not before mine honor: nor my Lusts
> Burne hotter than my Faith.

But here their godships are introduced in gently humorous fashion; and the same free spirit of "sweet-reasonableness" that thus lightly mocks one convention, will easily carry off such another, as in

> this hand
> As soft as Doves-downe, and as white as it,
> Or Ethyopians tooth, or the fan'd snow,
> That's bolted by the Northerne blasts twice ore;

making it young and fresh again. About the whole there is a lilt and delicacy which differentiates it completely from the earlier lyricism. This is partly due to the easy run of the verse, which seems to wander at its own sweet will, without needing to be coaxed or wrought into shape by the author. There are no Procrustean tactics used here. Where a resolution or feminine ending is necessary, it falls out naturally, without noisily asserting its independence and originality. The typical line is simple, fluent, lightly stressed:

> [Their transformations]
> Were never for a peece of beauty rarer,

and often this simplicity has a colloquial tinge:

> Nothing she do's, or seemes
> But smackes of something greater than herselfe,

or that more famous line from *The Tempest*:

> They'l take suggestion, as a Cat laps milke.

It is, I think, in this colloquialism that the real secret of this verse lies. It is the most natural verse that Shakspere has written; its tones and cadences are those of the human voice (which incidentally is perhaps the reason why "Shaksperian" actors find it so peculiarly hard to deliver). And yet it is an ideal human voice; the voice of a man passionless, untouched by everyday worry and change, at peace within himself.

As such it was no medium for tragedy. It could only be spoken by dwellers in a fairy-tale world, or better still, by the transcendental Prospero:

> We are such stuffe
> As dreams are made on: and our little life
> Is rounded with a sleepe.

It is all dream-stuff, this verse.

The immense difference between the pastoral poetry and what may be called the intrigue verse in these last plays makes the distinction between main-plot and sub-plot as emphatic as that between age and youth. When the smoother verse is introduced into an intrigue scene the contrast is, of course, all the more striking, and this constitutes an important dramatic effect. To take an early example: Antony's rough exuberance in the hour of victory has been already quoted, and in the first moments after his defeat he remains equally violent:

Vanish, or I shall give thee thy deserving,
And blemish Caesar's Triumph. Let him take thee,
And hoist thee up to the shouting Plebians
> etc. etc.

The sudden quietness of his despair is then all

the more ominous when expressed with such measured regularity as this:

> Sometime we see a clowd that's Dragonish,
> A vapour sometime, like a Beare, or Lyon,
> A tower'd Cittadell, a pendant Rocke,
> A forked Mountaine, or blew Promontorie
> With trees upon't, that nodde unto the world,
> And mocke our eyes with Ayre.

And there is exactly the same change of mood, depending upon the same change of verse-quality, between Leontes jealous, and Leontes penitent. In the first torment of his suspicion he cries: There have been

> (Or I am much deceiv'd) Cuckolds ere now,
> And many a man there is (even at this present,
> Now, while I speake this) holds his Wife by th' Arme,
> That little thinkes she ha's been sluyc'd in's absence,
> And his Pond fish'd by his next Neighbor (by
> Sir *Smile*, his Neighbor:)

But when the oracle has proved his jealousy to be unfounded, the knots and distortions fall from his speech, and his recovered sanity is expressed in verse deliberately formalised upon the old end-stopped pattern:

> Apollo pardon
> My great prophanenesse 'gainst thine Oracle.
> Ile reconcile me to *Polixenes*,

New woo my Queene, recall the good *Camillo*
(Whom I proclaime a man of Truth, of Mercy:)
etc. etc.

This brings me to the whole question of the
effects gained by placing different types of verse
side by side in the same play; and that must be
the subject of the next section.

## §2. CONTRASTS AND COMBINATIONS

The inequality of Shakspere's style has often dis-
concerted the more sensitive of his worshippers.
Scenes which open with admirably robust prose
slip aside into the quips and quibbles, the affected
gesturings and artificial graces of Euphuism; and
lines of the purest and most directly expressed
feeling give place to megaphone speeches which
the fine scholar condemns as bad art, the fine
gentleman as bad form. Even such a true
admirer as Dryden "cannot say he is everywhere
alike....He is many times flat and insipid; his
comick wit degenerating into clenches, his
serious swelling into bombast".

The early editors had an easy, but not wholly
satisfying way of dealing with this problem. The
parts which they approved they marked with

[ 75 ]

"commas, double commas, and asterisks"; and forgot, as well as they could, all but these elegant extracts. Modern critics, following the fashion set by Malone, appease their aesthetic conscience more completely by rejecting, as non-Shaksperian, any passage which they cannot praise. But though their signs of disapproval may differ, all are equally agreed that the works of Shakspere, as we have them, are very uneven.

Shakspere's predecessors and immediate contemporaries seem to have worked more carefully, or to have employed less unworthy collaborators; for nothing like Shaksperian variety is to be found in their plays. This is not to deny that their thought and feeling may be exceedingly variable in quality, or even that as fine examples of bombast and insipidity are to be discovered in their works as in those of Shakspere. There is however an affinity between their extremes; a basic style which may be now inflated into rhetoric, now deflated into the commonplace of conversation. It is possible to find a highest common factor for all the verse of each of the earlier Elizabethan dramatists. Marlowe and Kyd, Marston, Jonson, and Chapman have each a distinct style, which, though hard to define, is yet recognisably present throughout their work. Lesser playwrights, such as Peele and Greene, though they frequently imitate Marlowe, have nevertheless an individuality as great and as constant as their betters. In all, though mood and even language may change from time to time, the essential movement and cadence of the verse in any one play, as well as the aesthetic aim and method of its presentation, remain always the same.

Take for instance two passages from *Antonio and Mellida*. Here, in the first part, is Marston at his loudest and worst:

> Loe, the sea grewe mad,
> His bowels rumbling with winde passion,
> Straight swarthy darknesse popt out Phoebus eye,
> And blurd the jocund face of bright cheekt day;
> Whilst crudl'd fogges masked even darknesse brow:
> Heaven bad's good night, and the rocks gron'd
> At the intestine uprore of the maine.

and here, in the *Revenge*, in a mood of quiet sentimentality:

> With that her head sunk down upon her brest:
> Her cheeke chang'd earth, her senses slept in rest:
> Untill my foole, that press'd unto the bed,
> Screch'd out so lowd that he brought back her soule,

Calde her againe, that her bright eyes gan ope,
And starde upon him: He audatious foole,
Dar'd kisse her hand, wisht her soft rest, lov'd bride;
She fumbled out, thanks good, and so she dide.

These two are superficially very unlike; but it is
only a difference of mood and language that
makes them appear so. The flow of the verse
remains the same, governed by the unvarying
characteristic of Marston's work; which, if it
must be defined, may be called a studied literariness of style and picturesqueness of phrase, that
make even the fiercest of his tirades move at a
leisurely pace. This vigorous leisureliness is as
distinctive of Marston as is the triumphantly
sweeping phrase of Marlowe; or, to use Webster's
description, "the labor'd and understanding
workes" are of "Maister Johnson". And in the
same way Kyd's gentility underlies all the patterned utterances of the courtly personages in
the *Spanish Tragedy*, the "full and haightned stile
of Maister Chapman", both the bragging of
Bussy and the pedantry of his brother.

No such universal style is discoverable for
Shakspere. It is of course possible to say, as I
have been saying, that in a particular play verse
of a particular kind is predominant; and in the

rhetorical period Shakspere seems deliberately to
have attempted some sort of uniformity. But in
the later plays the verse usually differs in quality
as much between scene and scene, person and
person, as from drama to drama. It is interesting
to compare with the Marston passages quoted
above a parallel pair from *Othello*:

For do but stand upon the Foaming Shore,
The chidden Billow seemes to pelt the Clowds,
The winde-shak'd-surge, with high and monstrous
    Maine
Seemes to cast water on the burning Beare,
And quench the Guards of th' ever-fixed Pole.

This storm is fairly close to Marston's; but note
how, in a quieter scene, Marston is unable, or
unwilling, to forget his literariness, while Shakspere modulates to this:

My Mother had a Maid call'd *Barbarie*,
She was in love: and he she lov'd prov'd mad,
And did forsake her. She had a Song of Willough,
An old thing 'twas: but it express'd her Fortune,
And she dy'd singing it. That song to-night,
Will not go from my mind: I have much to do,
But to go hang my head all at one side
And sing it like poore *Barbarie*.

Leaving aside all differences of mood and language, no affinity can be found between Desde-

mona's homeliness and the high-sounding verse
of the second Cypriot gentleman, between the
limpid irregularity of "poore Barbarie's" story
and the highly stressed regularity of the storm-
description. And the aptness of the variations
to their subject-matter suggests that the Shaksperian unevenness is the result, not of unequal
inspiration or unwise partnership, but of a
dramatic method as studied and deliberate as
Jonson's cult of uniformity. This suggestion I
now propose to examine, taking first those kinds
of speech which deviate most widely from the
norm of the staple verse, namely prose and the
rhymed couplet.

## (a) Prose

The device of introducing prose as contrast
into a play in verse was used by other dramatists
beside Shakspere; although the most conscien-
tious of them, Chapman, and Jonson (if we
except the mountebank scene in *Volpone*), re-
nounced such a mingling of styles, at least in
serious plays. But in most Elizabethan drama
outside Shakspere the distinction between the
two harmonies is very clear-cut: verse is for the
nobility and gentry, while a conventional prose

is reserved for the low characters. Shakspere, on the other hand, uses prose as readily for courtiers off duty and noblemen distraught as for his clowns, and ranges from plain English to English Ciceronian, from Euphues to tavern-talk.

The conventional clown's prose—or rather that peculiar brand of it, exuberant and original, which Shakspere was always able to bestow upon his clowns from Launce to Stephano—is by no means the least common type of prose to appear in Shakspere's plays. Citizens, grave diggers, porter, gaoler, shepherds, Pompey and Lavache, the clown who runs Desdemona's errands, and the clown who brings Cleopatra the asp, all are in the tradition. And, closely allied to them are all those who, though ostensibly of a higher order, are yet denied the dignity of verse: Pandarus and Thersites whose minds are essentially beastly, Roderigo who has no mind at all; Enobarbus the blunt soldier, Kent and Casca who assume bluntness, the one as a disguise, the other merely as an effective pose; Cloten and Parolles whom Nature made buffoons, Lucio and Menenius who are themselves responsible for their own deliberate buffoonery.

In the prose of the last two can be seen traces

of another kind of usage (where, however, the main purpose is still a specifically comic relief) of which the chief example is "young Osricke": namely the studied caricature of current affectations of speech, which are naturally more easily reproducible in prose than in verse. It is important, nevertheless, to notice that Shakspere, except in the early plays, never exploits affectation for its own sake, as so many of his contemporaries did. Osrick's artificial conversation is the lull before the final storm of *Hamlet*. The equally affected interchange between the Court ushers, in the last act of *The Winter's Tale*, obviates a discovery scene at once difficult to write and too reminiscent of that already written for *Pericles*; and, in addition, affords a welcome interlude in a long sequence of not very exciting verse.

The prose, then, of Shakspere's plays, whatever its intrinsic quality and effect, is always introduced with the primary intention of providing a contrast, the strongest possible contrast, to the staple verse. In all the examples hitherto quoted the contrast is a double one, on the twin planes of language and of action: buffoon prose—or Euphuistic prose—sets off the staple verse beside it, and creates, at the same time, a prose character with the exactly parallel function of setting off the verse-speaking protagonists. The simple contrast, that is the plain verse-prose opposition without any overtones of character, is equally common; the most straightforward examples being the letters and proclamations—read matter—which appear as patches of prose in the verse representing the spoken word. Sometimes it is merely the distinction between a reading voice and the more spontaneous utterance of original speech, which is to be made; and then, prose ended, the verse resumes immediately and continues as before, unmodified by the interruption: Hamlet's three letters, that of Macbeth to his lady, Apollodorus' warning, all these and many others like them are inserted bodily into the stream of verse without in any way affecting it. Sometimes the prose patch will strongly influence what follows: Edmund's challenge, delivered by Herald, makes his fight with Edgar more a combat of chivalry than the usual battle-field meeting (such as that between Macbeth and Macduff), and their mutual defiance is correspondingly thin-lipped and precise. Similarly the formal indictment of

Hermione gives to the trial scene in *The Winter's Tale* that sense of business-like reality which is carried over into the true court-of-law pleading, more logical than impassioned, of the Queen herself.

The atmosphere of matter-of-factness is often created by this use of prose. The contrast between Brutus' plain sense and Antony's subtle rhetoric lies chiefly in the fact that Antony uses verse while Brutus' speech is couched in prose. In prose Brabantio and the Duke proceed from questioning Othello to affairs of state. In prose Regan and Gonerill, laying aside the feigned sentiment of verse, plot against Lear's happiness; and the business arrangements which recur throughout this play, the despatching of messengers and receiving of news, the intriguing, and preliminary contriving generally, are all conducted in prose. Finally it may be noted that in the same medium are largely conceived the wire-pullings of the Duke in *Measure for Measure*; though here its extraordinary artificiality and affectation suggest that its chief purpose is to reinforce the Duke's disguise—it is, in fact, a written sign representing a feigned voice.

Very similar to these uses is the employment

of prose to present the mere facts of an exposition, the historical data upon which a play, or an act of a play, is to be founded. The prose interchange between Kent and Gloucester sets the stage for *Lear*, as that between Archidamus and Camillo does for *The Winter's Tale*; and again in the latter play the interview between Camillo and Polixenes, another prose scene, lays the foundation of intrigue beneath the pastoral poetry of the fourth act. *Coriolanus* also contains two examples: the rather formal conversation of the cushion-laying officers—the formality caught, perhaps, from North's Plutarch—ushers in the solemn presentation of the hero to the assembled senate; and later the meeting between a Roman and a Volscian prepares for his revolt.

The multiplication of instances can only be tedious; but it is interesting just to glance at two expositions which, although of the same type as those already quoted, are yet in verse. The opening of *Cymbeline*, for instance, is a stock example of the presentation of data by discussion between first and second gentlemen—an obvious occasion for prose; but the data partly consist of the romantic "characters" of Imogen and her husband, and so must necessarily be given in verse. Again, in the first scene of *Othello*, prose would be doubly natural, both as the proper medium for a business exposition, and as the habitual form of Iago's conversations with Roderigo; but here prose is needed later for Iago's impatient dropping of the courtly mask, with "Zounds Sir: you are one of those that will not serve God, if the devill bids you"; so that the opening must again be verse, contrary to all expectation.

From business to relaxation, from formality to informality, may seem a long step. The two may be easily reconciled if it is remembered, first, that since in real life prose is the normal medium of conversation, its introduction into a verse play will have the main effect of added realism; and that relaxation is as real and everyday as business: secondly, that beside this main effect (and by no means conflicting with it) there exists another, due to the fact that prose appears less ordered than verse—the feeling that there is in a prose speech, as compared with one in verse, a certain lack of constraint, even of control. The two effects combine in those "conversation scenes", which are a blend of interlude and realistic sketch: the discussion in the course of which

Posthumus wagers with Iachimo (though this might rank as a scene of preparatory intrigue); the prattle of young Macduff; Volumnia's reception of her neighbour Valeria, and the ensuing gossip; or the banter with which the villains of *The Tempest*, when first cast on the island, receive Gonzalo's suggestions for its colonisation—and note how, the victims once asleep and the plotting begun, their speech immediately tautens into verse.

Other scenes there are in which the second effect of prose is the most important; prose speeches whose realism is irrelevant, but which suggest lack of control in the speaker. The obvious examples are the cases of madness. Hamlet and Edgar, feigning themselves mad, speak prose; and from the truly mad, Ophelia or Lear, sanity and verse slip away together. The same change comes upon Othello in his trance and subsequent frenzy, and upon Lady Macbeth in her sleep-walking fit. These are the extreme instances; but there are others less glaring. A drunken man, according to Feste, is like a madman; and the two forms of losing one's self-control are portrayed by the same means. The innovation which one cup has made in Cassio's wits is shown at once by his dropping into prose on Iago's first hint of relaxation; and in the prose drinking scene which follows, Iago's verse asides reveal him still completely self-possessed. The lover has also been compared with the madman. The prose, then, of Troilus, in his first meeting with Cressida, may be also of this type; and this queer, gabbling stuff, the unnatural dissertation on monsters, may be the manifestation in words of that lack of self-possession caused by shyness and inexperience.

Before leaving prose, it may be as well to add a reminder; to insist that in a verse play the chief importance of prose lies in its being diametrically opposed to verse. The use, or avoidance, of all the devices discussed above must depend largely on the general pattern of the play. Whether Shakspere was conscious of this pattern, how far he deliberately alternated verse scenes and prose, is, of course, an open question. But that his use of prose is at least partly governed by such considerations is apparent, if the admirable distribution of the prose patches (irrespective of their kind) is studied in *Hamlet, Troilus and Cressida, Measure for Measure*; in the first three acts of *Lear*, and in the first two and last two of *Coriolanus* (the third, containing what is really the central conflict of the play, is more intense, and prose therefore drops out altogether); and in the last two acts of *Winter's Tale*. In all these the chief purpose of the prose is, as stated above, to provide a contrast, the strongest possible contrast, to the staple verse.

## (b) The couplet

If prose is the most informal shape which the dramatic speech of the Elizabethans can take, the couplet is the most formal. Not that Shakspere's contemporaries always used it as such; there is many a sequence of couplets, many an incidental rhyme, which appears for no other reason save that the author happens to be in the rhyming vein. And even Shakspere, in the earlier plays, will often introduce couplets with no greater justification, though he has already found a more definite use for them on occasion; to point a set of wit well played, or to create a quiet, unemotional atmosphere, whether courtly or pastoral.

To the other dramatists there was really only one situation which seemed to demand the couplet-form. A rhymed line is more memorable than a plain one; and so the favourite maxims, proverbs, and "sentences" were usually expressed in couplets—the rhyme in spoken speech achieving the same purpose, of calling attention to the sentiment, which in the printed editions was served by pointing hands or inverted commas. So also the lines marking the end of a scene or a forceful exit, even when not, as they so often are, proverbial, yet required a similar emphasis, and achieved it by the same method. In the plays of Webster, for example, where the characters are all more or less forceful, constantly flinging off the stage with a threat or a sneer to do or die, the recurrence of these exit couplets creates a pattern which is perhaps too intrusive.

Shakspere's use of the couplet is nothing like so crude. For one thing, his characters make their exits with less of a gesture. There are of course exceptions. Shakspere, if he chose, could be as melodramatic as the best, and in that mood he gave to Cymbeline's Queen the villainous couplets of her asides, to the tempted Pisanio a fit of righteous rhyming that might leave the audience, at the end of the scene, reassured of his integrity. But for the most part he reserves the exit couplet for those parting shots which are deliberately, even comically, flamboyant, as Pompey's

> Whip me? No, no, let Carman whip his Jade,
> The valiant heart's not whipt out of his trade.

This, it may be observed, occurs in a scene not of blank verse but of prose, a context which heightens still more its artificiality.

Again, Shakspere's moral reflections never appear in trite isolation; whether developed at musing length, or fatalistically curt as the famous sayings in *Lear*, they are always wrought in with the general thought of the play, having references and implications which could not exist in the stock "sentences" introduced with such smug finality by most other Elizabethan dramatists. It is perhaps necessary to make a distinction between Shakspere's own moralising, and that of his characters. His schemers, in particular, from the virtuous Helena to Cressida, her opposite, have a habit of fortifying themselves in their plans by means of sententious resolutions, often no more than popular saws and common proverbs which demand the formalised setting of rhyme. To this class presumably belongs the strange Coriolanus who tries to argue himself into continuing his undignified petitioning of the people's votes—a sequence of six couplets.

Cressida herself offers one of the most interesting examples. It has often been supposed that, in giving the form of rhymed verse to her only two soliloquies (the one explaining her motives in putting off Troilus, the other her regrets at deserting him), Shakspere was providing a deliberate indication of her fundamental falsity. This may, at least, be an additional purpose governing the choice of the couplet-form here; for in the same play there certainly seems to be a flavour of insincerity in Aeneas' rhymed mocking of the Greek generals, and in Cressida's own encounter with them, again a succession of couplets. These latter scenes are, of course, no more than revivals of the rhymed wit-contests so common in Shakspere's early plays; a fact that has led many a critic to assign these also to an early date. But with Shakspere, above all writers, the use of primitive methods does not necessarily imply a primitive stage of technical development. If the effects he required could best be achieved by primitive methods, he was not afraid to use them at any stage in his career. In Cressida's soliloquies the proverbial couplets

[ 92 ]

are apparently used to suggest insincerity; elsewhere in the play the convention of the wit-contest is adapted to create the same sense of superficiality. And in *All's Well*, Helen's rhymed conversation with the King, or, more strikingly, with the lords proposed as her suitors (another "early" scene), is only a different adaptation of the same convention; this time the couplets produce a deliberate formalisation of the unlikely elements in the story, comparable with that obtained in *The Merchant of Venice* by more violent means. Couplets, in short, have now reached that degree of stylisation which, in the earlier play, was occupied by stanza-forms and other than decasyllabic verse.

Stylisation is one of the most obvious effects of Rhyme, when it appears in the mature plays, and its artificiality is often directly referred to in the context. There is, for instance, that strange scene in the last act of *Cymbeline*, where Posthumus taunts a coward lord, as Aeneas the Greeks, in couplets, which he introduces with the words "Will you Rime upon 't, And vent it for a Mock'rie?" and again "You have put me into Rime". So too Iago prepares the audience for his rhymed characters with "my Muse labours,

and thus she is deliver'd". This conscious isolation of rhymed verse from its surroundings is
used to best advantage in Hamlet's Mouse-trap,
where the couplet-form keeps the play-within-
the-play markedly distinct from the play proper;
and similarly in *The Winter's Tale* the rhyming
speech of Time differentiates that inhuman prologue from the more real characters.

With regard to the last example, it may be
noticed that Time's speech contains the only
couplets in the whole of the play. The compact
body of rhyme, sharply dividing the tragic story
from the comedy, is an important landmark in the
play's progression, an outward symbol defining
the dramatic structure beneath. This structural
use of the couplet is one of the most important
employments to which Shakspere put it, and is
seldom found in the work of his contemporaries
except in such crude forms as the Websterian
pattern of exits already noticed. Shakspere can
make use of it on a small scale, in a single scene,
to point the stages of an argument; of that the
Trojan council of war in *Troilus and Cressida* provides an admirably written example. Or he can
use it to mark each movement in the dramatic
progression of a whole play, as in *Macbeth*. Here

a large proportion of the scenes end with a couplet, a pair of couplets, or two couplets with only a single line dividing them, and these closing rhymes give a sense of finality to each successive step which Macbeth takes toward his own ruin; with every deed signed and sealed by a couplet there can be no retraction. Shakspere, in short, often uses the couplet as a full-close in music; sometimes, as in *Macbeth*, it is quietly made, without a flourish; sometimes it is brayed out with the full strength of trumpet and drum. The couplet-sequences with which Kent and Cordelia mark their departure from Lear's court reveal the King's first errors as terrifyingly final and irremediable; and at the end of the play (there are few rhymed lines in the interim) the completeness of the catastrophe, and the feeling of hopelessness, of exhaustion in which the surviving characters are left, are clinched and set in the final sequence of four couplets. None other of the tragedies, it may be remarked, has more than two—*Romeo and Juliet* has a stanza, which produces the quite different effect of rounding off the story, of reducing it to that formality and orderliness prescribed for it by the opening sonnet. And in none of the other tragedies is there this feeling of exhaustion, of no hope for the future, which is present in *Lear*. Denmark may well become a great and noble state under the Kingship of Fortinbras, Venice survives, a great sea-power still, after the death of Othello, and Antony's fate gives, somehow, new energy and surety to the massive progress of the Roman Empire, ever present behind the action of the play. Only in Lear is all life and hope gone, all passion spent—a formal expiration that receives its appropriate expression in the couplet-sequence.

In the first act of *Othello* the whole orchestra, both rhyme and prose, is employed in emphasising the full-close. After Brabantio has at last granted his consent to the marriage of Othello and Desdemona, the Duke, in his own words, "lays a Sentence, which as a grise, or step may help these Lovers into your favour". This sentence is a series of four proverbs each expressed in a couplet; Brabantio caps them with five more, making an unbroken sequence of nine couplets. This measured sententiousness sets a formidable seal upon the now irrevocable marriage; Brabantio's abrupt change of subject with "humbly beseech you proceed to th' Affairs of State", and

[ 96 ]

the Duke's business prose, mentioned in the last section, together close the last loophole. What's done cannot be undone. The fatal step is taken, and we await the inevitable advance of destiny. Such is the new effectiveness which Shakspere could give to the dullest of conventional usages.

### (c) Bombast

Bombast is a vague term, and I wish it to remain so. I use it here to cover everything which a reader may find extravagant or unnatural—either language and sonority too great for the thought, or thought too great for the occasion. Its usual characteristics will be sounding apostrophes, to the sun, the heavens, the elements, virtues, vices, and gods; exaggerated wishes, and ranted resolutions. And it will include the self-consciously poetical whenever that is carried to such lengths as to make the reader uneasily critical.

The perspicacious will already have realised that here is another convention to be dealt with, a poetical convention that is peculiarly Elizabethan: namely the twin traditions of Senecan tragedy and Petrarchan lyricism. It is, in fact, the intrusion of what in an earlier section I have called the heaven-battle-thunder-devils and rose-lily-ivory-and-gold styles of poetry into Shakspere's mature work, that is now to be studied. But though Senecanism and Petrarchism were very real conventions, they are not so easily marked down in a blank-verse field as the more obviously heterogeneous prose and rhyme. Consequently the most serious difficulty of this examination lies in the fact that a great part of the data must depend on personal taste and ear. The grosser kinds of bombast will probably be admitted by all readers; but passages of less blatantly bad rhetoric, or of less painfully artificial lyricism, will be found hollow by one, and satisfying, equally justifiably, by another. Again, lines condemned as bombastic when studying a play may become perfectly convincing when spoken on the stage, where they are carried through by the drive of the action and the personality of the actor. But though the emotional excitement of actual representation may blur the distinctions, it does not destroy them. A change of verse-quality may still be recognised, though not so striking here in the theatre as it formerly appeared in the library.

It may very well be asked whether the Elizabethans themselves would have noticed a change from Shakspere to Seneca, and if so whether they would have attached any peculiar dramatic or emotional significance to it. The answer to the second question must be deduced from this whole subsection; and that they could feel the change in tone, is, I think, certain. There are constant references which prove that they did recognise, and resent, extravagance in the language or movement of a speech. Even as early as in *King John*, written within a year or two of Marlowe's death, we find the Bastard greeting the defiance uttered by the citizens of Angiers—and it is not wildly extravagant as defiances go—with the words:

> Here's a large mouth indeede,
> That spits forth death, and mountaines, rockes, and
> seas,
> Talkes as familiarly of roaring Lyons,
> As maids of thirteene do of puppi-dogges.

Hamlet's famous directions to the players are, of course, much more explicit in their condemnation of extravagance. And if Shakspere's testimony is suspected, on the ground that he was abnormally sensitive in this respect, there is Jonson's ridicule of the high-flown language of Marston; even

Marston himself, in the induction to *Antonio and Mellida*, makes one character remark, upon the bombast of another, "Rampum scrampum, mount tuftie *Tamburlaine*. What rattling thunderclappe breakes from his lips". If Marston, himself a sinner, could react to it thus, it is improbable that the Elizabethan audience remained unmoved.

One use of bombast, certainly, the Elizabethans must have recognised, coming, as it did, of such an old and great tradition. In Greek tragedy violent action on the stage was prohibited; the major catastrophes were made known by means of a messenger, and to him were given a formalism and pretentiousness of phrase which might be some substitute for the impressiveness of a witnessed disaster. This practice was copied in Seneca's tragedies, a form of drama in which there was even less action than in the Greek, and from Seneca passed to his English imitators. Thereafter even those playwrights who professed to despise the classicists and who, by introducing horrors on the stage itself, had forfeited the excuse of their predecessors, would still use the wordy messenger as a useful convention; and the English messenger is nearer related to the Greek than to those fellow-countrymen who have not his office. Even the least conscious of his obligations has that stiltedness which can announce a death in the words "He ceased to be a man"; and this same stiltedness, magnified, can become the almost incredible pomposity of the messenger in *Bussy d'Ambois*:

> What Atlas, or Olympus lifts his head
> So farre past covert, that with aire enough
> My words may be inform'd?

Shakspere's messenger, though his mouth is not as large as that of Chapman's "passionate and waighty Nuntius", is no exception to the general rule. The messengers who announce Gloucester's fate in *Lear*, and the Turkish attack in *Othello*, have the characteristic formality and prim extravagance; but the best examples are, as might be expected, from the Roman plays, particularly *Antony and Cleopatra*. In the messenger speeches of this play are to be found specimens not only of the formal Senecan sentiment, as

> The nature of bad newes infects the teller,

but also of the more truly bombastic shape which

this formality takes when the news is urgent.
The speech of a courier to Caesar:

*Menacrates* and *Menas* famous Pyrates
Make the sea serve them, which they eare and wound
With keeles of every kinde,

struts and postures as much as any in the play.

With the messengers who are actually so
called must, of course, be taken all those to whom
the office of reporting news falls at any time. The
appalling change which comes upon a normal
character who undertakes this duty is admirably
shown in Jonson's *Sejanus*: there Terentius, a
minor personage of hitherto blameless speech,
suddenly assumes the Senecan rhetoric to announce Sejanus' death. Something of the same
sort happens to the Scarus of *Antony and Cleopatra*, who is, however, by nature more inclined
to high language; but even a flamboyant nature
will hardly excuse this account of Cleopatra's
flight:

ENO.                    How appears the fight?
SCAR.    On our side like the token'd pestilence,
Where death is sure. Yon ribaudred nag of Egypt,
(Whom leprosie o're-take) i'th' midst o'th' fight,
When vantage like a payre of Twinnes appear'd

Both as the same, or rather ours the elder;
(The Breeze upon her) like a Cow in June,
Hoists Sailes, and flyes.

A very close parallel, in energy and movement,
to Scarus' speech is that of the bloody sergeant
in *Macbeth*, which reaches such height of bombast that it has been rejected by several critics
as non-Shaksperian. Whether Shakspere wrote
it or no, it seems to me to have a very important
influence upon the play, and I shall reconsider it
later in more detail.

Both the sergeant and Scarus are in these
speeches nothing more than messengers dis-
guised. Their verse is not primarily an index to
personality. The gentleman who, in *Hamlet*,
announces Laertes' rebellion, is even more impersonal:

The Ocean (over-peering of his List)
Eates not the Flats with more impittious haste
Then young *Laertes*, in a Riotous head,
Ore-beares your Officers
etc. etc.

It is interesting to find that the good Gentleman
of the modern editions is, in the Folio, plain
Messenger.

A caution must be entered against attributing

messenger bombast entirely to the Senecan tradition. The subject of these announcements is generally either sudden death or war; and each of these is often alone guilty of inciting to bombast. It is possible that all Shakspere's messenger speeches, though their pomposity is conveniently derived all the way from the Greek, should more properly be divided between the two classes of bombast which are next to be considered.

First, sudden death. There is no set speech for Horror. The discoverer of the body is usually inarticulate, or at least incoherent, and his emotions are more likely to be expressed in violent action than in a torrent of words. Unfortunately the inarticulate and the violently active are the two modes of behaviour which are least effective on the stage; hence Horror must be represented symbolically, through some convention of speech which shall always convey this speechless emotion.

In Shakspere the symbol is usually bombast, and, at a lower emotional tension, that formal artificiality which has already appeared as akin to it. Macduff's reaction to the murder of Duncan is a good example of this use: "O horror,

horror, horror", he cries, "Tongue nor Heart cannot conceive, nor name thee"; but they nevertheless proceed immediately to make the attempt, as follows:

> Confusion now hath made his Master-peece:
> Most sacrilegious Murther hath broke ope
> The Lords anoynted Temple, and stole thence
> The Life o' th' Building.
> Approch the Chamber, and destroy your sight
> With a new *Gorgon*.
>
> etc. etc.

This is not a time for elaborate allusions to the divine right of Kings, or to classical mythology; but Macduff's extravagance of speech is accepted as symbolising the disorder of his mind.

Minor characters are more composed, but no less conventional, in similar situations. The Elizabethans were doubtless readier to accept sudden death philosophically than are their modern descendants; but there is more than human self-possession in the "Alack", "The gods forfend!" "O heavy day", and similar exclamations, with which the bystanders receive the deaths of Desdemona, Othello, Cordelia, Lear, Antony, Cleopatra, Coriolanus, and Hermione. This artificiality often takes the form of punning. Beside Juliet's famous "I", when she supposes Romeo dead, there is the cry of her namesake in *Measure for Measure*, on hearing the sentence passed upon her lover:

> Must die to-morrow? Oh injurious Love
> That respits me a life, whose very comfort
> Is still a dying horror.

This is almost the only passage that rings false in a play where the verse (the prose is another matter) is remarkably even.

Compare with these Lady Macbeth's:

> If he doe bleed,
> Ile guild the Faces of the Groomes withall,
> For it must seeme their Guilt,

Antony's quibble on "heart" and "hart" (a favourite one) over the dead Julius Caesar, and his punning when he supposes Cleopatra dead:

> now
> All length is Torture: since the Torch is out,
> Lye downe and stray no farther,

and many others. Most striking of all is perhaps Lodovico's comment, "Oh bloody period" (as Othello concludes his speech with his own death-stroke), where the pun and the conventional ejaculation combine. In all these the pun is a formal climax symbolising that emotional climax which cannot be expressed in words.

One passage alone appears at first sight to portray the incoherent agitation of the horror-struck in real life. In the last scene of *Lear* a Gentleman enters with a bloody knife, and this follows:

GENT. Helpe, helpe: O helpe.
EDG.                    What kinde of helpe?
ALB.                        Speake man.
EDG.  What means this bloody knife?
GENT.                        'Tis hot, it smoakes,
It came even from the heart of—O she's dead.
ALB.  Who dead? Speake man.

It was, however, a desire not for realism but for dramatic effect that produced this. The stuttering horror of the gentleman keeps the audience in greater suspense. Like Albany, they are desperate to know who actually is dead. They fear for Cordelia; their relief, at hearing that it is only Gonerill gone, is correspondingly great, and they are thus raised to a pitch of security which makes the final disaster all the more unexpected and terrible. Studied in isolation, without the

[ 107 ]

support of this continuous suspense, the behaviour of the gentleman is comic, as indeed its counterpart in real life would be, without the support of reality. It is probably for this reason that Shakspere does not repeat the experiment in situations of less emotional tension, but relies upon the bombastic convention which had served him so well from the supposed death of Juliet onwards.

The bombast of horror and sudden death belongs most properly to the convention of Senecan rhetoric; that of war and warriors, now to be considered, is most closely allied to the heroics of Marlowe, which represent the other great rhetorical tradition in Elizabethan drama.

The Tamburlaine type evidently appealed to Shakspere, as to his contemporaries. The histories are full of examples, broadened perhaps, and anglicised, but still recognisable. The warrior Talbot is markedly more boisterous than his companions. The Bastard, in *King John*, softened a little by his sense of humour, has yet for his motto, "Threaten the threateners, and outface the brow of bragging horror". Hotspur continues the line, and utters some notable Tamburlainisms, as in the famous honour-speech, and this, less frequently quoted:

> let them come,
> They come like Sacrifices in their trimme,
> And to the fire-ey'd Maid of smoakie warre,
> All hot, and bleeding, will wee offer them:
> The mayled *Mars* shall on his Altar sit
> Up to the eares in blood.

Finally, in *Henry V*, the warrior-hero becomes a main figure of the play, and so prepares for the great heroes of the tragedies, Othello, Antony, and Coriolanus. But, before considering these three in more detail, it is proper to examine the purpose of this rhetoric.

Large voices have been popularly attributed to soldiers from the time of Homer, and presumably before. Furthermore the military braggart has been a favourite subject for the stage ever since the example was first given by the Greek prototypes of Thraso and Pyrgopolinices. The Elizabethan hero does not, however, brag for realistic, or for comic effect. It is improbable that Queen Elizabeth's generals did in fact stalk about the battle-field crying "I am the sonne of Marcus Cato, hoe", or "Turne, Hell-hound turne". That their counterparts in Shakspere's plays do so is due, partly perhaps to the tradition of chivalry as preserved in literature, more to the fact, alluded to before, that stage action can express only a very limited activity. The final medium is always speech. The desperate energy and excitement of a battle-field cannot be shown in the movements of three or four actors on a few square yards of staging, but must be translated into a corresponding fury of speech. Similarly the stage does not afford sufficient scope for the man of action to reveal himself in deeds. His promptness, his vigour, his strength of arm as well as his strength of will, must appear in his language. Drama has no place for the strong, and silent, man.

This is exemplified, at its simplest, in the wordy warfare which accompanies, if it does not actually replace, the physical combats of Hector and Ajax, Macbeth and Macduff, Aufidius and Coriolanus. The same device, on a larger scale, is used to create the atmosphere of war which dominates the play of *Troilus and Cressida*. The stage is set in a superbly fulsome prologue, spoken by an armed man:

> In Troy there lyes the scene: From Iles of Greece
> The princes Orgillous, their high blood chaf'd,
> Have to the Port of Athens sent their shippes

Fraught with the ministers and instruments
Of cruell Warre:

and again:

Priam's six-gated city,
*Dardan* and *Timbria, Helias, Chetas, Troien,*
And *Antenorides* with massie staples
And corresponsive and fulfilling Bolts
Sperre up the sonnes of Troy.

Note here the combination of rich phraseology,
the Marlovian trick of using full-sounding
names, and the massy Latinisms which are to
persist throughout the play. The effect is to
emphasise at once the strife of nations which
might else have been forgotten in the com-
paratively light and artificial scenes of the love
story which open the play proper.

The war scenes sustain the note set by the
prologue and present the two traditional warrior
types in opposition. On the one side the Miles
Gloriosus is reincarnated in the braggarts
Achilles and Ajax (the mocking of Pyrgopolinices
by his slave might be the model for the scene in
which the Greek generals humour Ajax to his
face, deride him behind his back). Of the rest,
Nestor is the comic old bore whom Shakspere so
often introduces; and Agamemnon's pomposity

[ 111 ]

is to reappear in the Romans of *Antony and Cleo-patra*. Only Ulysses and Diomed, slightly more imaginative, escape this taint; for most of Ulysses' rodomontade is a mock of his fellows, as:

Besides the applause and approbation
To which, most mighty for thy place and sway
And thou most reverend for thy stretcht-out life,
I give to both your speeches: which were such,
As *Agamemnon* and the hand of Greece
Should hold up high in Brasse: and such againe
As venerable *Nestor* (hatch'd in Silver)
Should with a bond of ayre, strong as the Axle tree
In which the Heavens ride, knit all Greekes eares
To his experienc'd tongue:
etc. etc.

Yet even Ulysses, with his perpetual plottings and his proverbs, has moments of conventionality and humourlessness.

On the other side is Troilus, the "parfit gentil knight", and Hector, who spares his opponents in battle, sends challenges in correct chivalric form, and even attains the true Marlovian ring in such lines as:

Not Neoptolymus so mirable,
On whose bright crest, fame with her lowdst (Oyes)
Cries, This is he; could'st promise to himselfe
A thought of added honor, torne from *Hector*.

[ 112 ]

The individual heroes are however unimportant beside the general heroism of the play. The various combinations of brag and bombast create the effect of great warriors in action, and in this, at least, the play is truly Homeric.

Of the three great Tamburlaines in Shakspere's tragedies Coriolanus, though the latest in date, is the simplest. The same atmosphere of war and of great deeds as in *Troilus* pervades this play also, but its sole purpose here is to support the central character. The other soldiers of the play are little more than the aura of Coriolanus himself. There are constant descriptions, in hyperbolical language, of the hero, and of his feats. Something of the same method Shakspere had used in *Julius Caesar*; but there the inhuman greatness of Julius is shown rather by hints and chance phrases. Caesar would "soar above the view of men", "get the start of the majesticke world", "bestride the narrow world like a Colossus". The puffing of Coriolanus is more direct. Menenius, Volumnia, Lartius, Cominius, all give him extravagant praise; his enemy Aufidius calls him "thou Mars", and cries:

Let me twine
Mine armes about that body, where against

My grained Ash an hundred times hath broke,
And scarr'd the Moone with splinters.

As with Julius, even the taunts of his de-
tractors are couched in such fulsome verse that
they only heighten his glory:

Being mov'd, he will not spare to gird the Gods,
Bemocke the modest Moone,

comment the tribunes after Marcius' first appearance; and later Brutus' high-flown denunciation
of the popular enthusiasm emphasises the climax
of the hero's fame.

All these characters merely buttress with their
high words the nobility of Coriolanus and his
mother, already established in the bombast of
their own speeches. Volumnia is as loud-voiced
as her son—indeed, as she herself says, bravado
is hereditary among the Marcii; "thy Valiant-
nesse was mine, thou suck'st it from me".
Coriolanus himself has been called a "melodious
megaphone"; and certainly his speeches have an
easy sonority, and a luxuriance of "protest, of
oath, and big compare", that become monotonous. This is, however, a perfectly successful
representation, stylised certainly, but coherent,
of the man of action pure and simple, without

[ 114 ]

humour or imagination. Coriolanus is Shakspere's Tamburlaine, but without a Zenocrate,
and as such is convincing. If we quarrel with the
play it must be on the grounds, not of inadequate
characterisation, but that the plain man of action,
however well represented, does not provide
good material for the drama.

Tamburlaine receives his Zenocrate, and the
redeeming imagination that perhaps goes with
her, in *Othello*. But the exaltation of the hero is
in this play achieved by means exactly opposite
to those used for Coriolanus. He, a Roman
among Romans, owes his grandeur to the fact
that he is at once the greatest, and most Roman,
of them all; Othello, a black-skinned Moor amid
fair Venetians, is colossal in, and through,
his isolation. The lesser voices of *Coriolanus* are
echoes, reverberations rather, of the hero's; in
*Othello* their simplicity is sharply contrasted with
his richness. For nothing is more mistaken than
to apply such terms as the music of Othello,
appropriate to the Moor himself, to the whole
play.

Cassio certainly can become self-consciously
poetical when describing Desdemona; but this
rhapsody, closely paralleled by that of Enobarbus

over Cleopatra, is intended to exalt the praised
rather than the praiser. It is another example of
the puff by bombast. The description of the
storm in the same scene is highly bombastic also;
but this has, I believe, a dramatic purpose quite
distinct from character-drawing, and will be
considered in a later section. Apart from these
exceptions, the ground bass to the Othello music
is straightforward verse, unadorned almost to
bareness. The contrast between the imaginative
Moor and the homely Desdemona is made
admirably effective in their verse; and Iago,
whose natural exuberance is betrayed by the
extraordinary richness of his prose relaxations,
assumes as his disguise a plain-spokenness which
emphasises his opposition to Othello.

Of the hero himself it must be remembered
that he is a foreigner. It is a mistake to see in him
merely the Elizabethan soldier painted black.
Throughout the play the fact that he is an alien,
sharply divided from his fellows by race and
colour, is constantly insisted upon. Othello is a
Moor; and the Moor of the Elizabethan stage,
from Aaron to the villain-hero of *All's Lost by
Lust*, was a very constant and recognisable type.
Since the seventeenth century, the reputation for

extravagant emotionalism and unaccountable changes of mood has left the Moors, and passed farther east. It is as an Oriental, in the widest and most romantic sense, a man incalculable and exotic, of strange mystical passions, suddenly inspired, that Othello must be studied to-day.

This view of the Moor explains not only his luminous phrases and sensuous imagery, not only the extraordinary glamour of his traveller's tales, of the "antars vast and desarts idle", but also his strange frenzies:

> Whip me ye Divels,
> From the possession of this Heavenly sight:
> Blow me about in windes, roast me in Sulphure,
> Wash me in steepe-downe gulfes of Liquid Fire.
> Oh Desdemona! Desdemona! dead!
> Oh! Oh! Oh!

The last lines—even more incoherent in the Folio—recall Thomson's "O Sophonisba, Sophonisba O", and the "waggish parody" that was made upon it. And yet here they are completely convincing as the representation of that lack of emotional restraint which the European expects, and distrusts, in the Savage, however Noble.

In Antony, the third of Shakspere's great

soldiers, such extravagances seem less spontaneous than in either of the others; and the problem is here to decide how far they are serious, how far an affectation. The persons of *Antony and Cleopatra*, like those of *Troilus and Cressida*, are divided into two camps; the Roman *gravitas*, dour, formal and completely without humour, is opposed to the *illiberalitas* of the Alexandrian court, languid, luxurious and insincere. The Romans are pompous by nature, the Egyptians in mockery of pomposity; to which side does Antony truly belong?

Consider the first scene. The play opens with an expression of the Roman spirit in the fulsome disgust of the veteran Philo. As he finishes, Antony and Cleopatra enter; they are exchanging the banter of courtly love in a sophisticated and perfunctory way, and Antony seems quite competent to match the Queen:

> CLEO. If it be love indeed, tell me how much.
> ANT. There's beggery in the love that can be reckon'd.
> CLEO. Ile set a bourne how farre to be belov'd.
> ANT. Then must thou needes finde out new Heaven, new Earth.

The messenger interrupts, and Cleopatra teases

Antony, who dismisses Rome, turning to her with these words:

> Let Rome in Tyber melt, and the wide Arch
> Of the raing'd Empire fall.

This is fulsome, if not bombastic; and it is questionable whether Antony is here the Roman in oratorical mood, or, with the Egyptians, a mocker of Rome's greatness.

There can be no doubt that Shakspere intended Antony to be a hero just as Coriolanus is a hero. The method of emphasising Antony's heroic qualities indeed anticipates that used for Coriolanus, or rather, since Antony is shown the more colossal of the two, Coriolanus borrows the device from the earlier play. There is scarcely a person, friend or foe, who does not allude to Antony's mighty soldiership in more or less extravagant terms. It is "twice the other twaine" (Pompey); his name is "that magicall word of warre" (Ventidius), and in it lies "a moity of the world" (Caesar); he should "answer like himselfe...as lowd as Mars" (Enobarbus), and in his noble countenance "the worship of the whole world lyes" (Eros); he is the "demy Atlas of this earth (Cleopatra), "still a Jove" (a soldier of Caesar), "the crowne o' th' earth" (Cleopatra), and many more, ranging between the "plated Mars" of Philo, and the colossal figure of the dream which Cleopatra tells to Dolabella:

> His face was as the Heav'ns, and therein stucke
> A Sunne and Moone, which kept their course,
>     and lighted
> This little O, the earth. . . .
> His legges bestrid the Ocean, his rear'd arme
> Crested the world, etc.

Antony himself, in defeat or victory, is full of the bombastic phrases proper to a hero. "I will appeare in blood", "I and my sword will earne our chronicle", "I will be trebble-sinewed, hearted, breath'd", "Ile set my teeth, and send to darknesse all that stop me", "Ile force the wine peepe through their scarres", "Ile make death love me, for I will contend even with his pestilent scythe"; all these occur within twenty lines of each other. Later success inspires lines with the genuine Tamburlaine ring, so that the "jolly march. . .through Alexandria" recalls the ". . .ride in triumph through Persepolis"; and there are a number of highly coloured self-portraits—"a workman. . .in the royall occupation", "a man of steel", "the pine...that overtop'd them all", "I, that with my Sword Quarter'd the World and o're greene Neptune's backe with Ships made Cities", "the greatest Prince o' th' world, the Noblest".

And yet Antony's worst bravado is subtly different from that of Coriolanus. Braggadocio is Coriolanus' natural language, and he can slip into ordinary conversation a picturesque phrase, such as "hornes o' th' Moone", which Antony screams out only as his nerves snap in the agony of his betrayal. Compare the two generals leading their forces into battle. Coriolanus:

> Advance brave *Titus*,
> They do disdaine us much beyond our Thoughts,
> Which makes me sweat with wrath,

and Antony:

> This Morning, like the spirit of a youth
> That meanes to be of note, begins betimes.

Compare, too, their epitaphs. A lord speaks this for Coriolanus:

> Let him be regarded
> As the most Noble Coarse, that ever Herald
> Did follow to his Urne.

And Caesar, when the news of Antony's death is brought to him, says:

> The death of *Anthony*
> Is not a single doome, in the name lay
> A moity of the world.

Look on this picture, and on this. The one is of a Juggernaut, the other of a Jupiter.

From pomp to pomposity the transition is easy. The Agamemnon of *Troilus and Cressida* has something of either; for he is both a part of the general warrior background of the play, and also the first representative of the Greek feudalism and humourlessness that is opposed to the chivalry and *joie de vivre* of the Trojans. As such he is held up to ridicule in Ulysses' parody already quoted; and his pomposity is comically emphasised in the reply:

> Speak Prince of *Ithaca*, and be't of lesse expect:
> That matter needlesse of importlesse burthen
> Divide thy lips; then we are confident
> When ranke *Thersites* opes his Masticke jawes,
> We shall heare Musicke, Wit, and Oracle.

He calls for a trumpeter with something of the same flourish as does Ajax:

> AGA.     With starting courage,
> Give with thy Trumpet a loud note to Troy

Thou dreadfull *Ajax*, that the appauled aire
May pierce the head of the great Combatant,
And hale him hither.

AJAX.　　　　　Thou, Trumpet, ther's my purse;
Now cracke thy longs, and split thy brazen pipe:
Blow villaine, till thy sphered Bias cheeke
Out-swell the collicke of puft *Aquilon*:
Come, stretch thy chest, and let thy eyes spout
　　blood:
Thou blowest for *Hector*.

But Agamemnon's rodomontade has not even
the gusto which enlivens that of the "mungrel
beef-witted lord"; his verse is for the most part
highly wrought without either the freedom of a
true hero's swinging rhythm, or the intellectual
drive that carries through the speeches of
Ulysses.

Of the Agamemnon type is the Octavius
Caesar of *Antony and Cleopatra*. The same warrior
atmosphere that was created for *Troilus and
Cressida* by the prologue pervades this play, from
the opening speech of the moral Roman, Philo;
but this militarism, though it is again a per-
manently felt background, is yet confined to one
of the opposing parties, to Rome and the
Empire, of which Caesar is the figure-head, as
Agamemnon of the sordid Achaeans.

[ 123 ]

Some of Caesar's bombastic speeches have a double purpose. Take, for instance, that spoken to the peace-maker Octavia, which Doctor Johnson found the most tumid in the play:

> The wife of *Anthony*
> Should have an Army for an Usher, and
> The Neighes of Horse to tell of her approach,
> Long ere she did appeare. The trees by th'way
> Should have borne men, and expectation fainted,
> Longing for what it had not. Nay, the dust
> Should have ascended to the Roofe of Heaven,
> Rais'd by your populous Troopes.

This may be taken as a glorification of the action, by reminding the audience of its setting—the Roman Empire in all its vastness and dignity. More important, it is a puff of Antony, just as the speeches of Cominius exalt Coriolanus, or Cassio's eulogy Desdemona. Yet at the same time, like all the other utterances of Caesar, it gives just that impression of slightly ridiculous self-importance which appeared in those of Agamemnon. The verse of Caesar throughout, seldom bombast of the Tamburlaine type, is all the more unconvincing in that its tumidity is unsupported by any sonority of phrase, or imaginative beauty. Of striking imagery even,

with a few such exceptions as the famous "vaga-
bond flagge upon the streame", there is none;
and the whole effect is of inflated commonplace.

Caesar's bombast, debased yet lower, becomes
the formality and long-windedness of that
favourite Shaksperian character, the foolish-
wise old councillor. Each of the two plays mentioned in the present section contains a specimen
of the type. Lepidus the triumvir proves his
kinship with Polonius by his behaviour at the
banquet, and at the same time retains something
of the Caesarian tumidity in his elaborate ex-
hortations and good wishes. Nestor, perhaps
owing to his warrior environment, is still more
fulsome. His proverbs and moralisings are
expressed in very high-flown verse:

...let the Ruffian *Boreas* once engage
The gentle *Thetis*, and anon behold
The strong ribb'd Barke through liquid Mountaines
    cut,
Bounding betweene the two moyst Elements
Like *Perseus*' Horse. Where's then the saucy Boate,
Whose weake untimber'd sides but even now
Co-rival'd Greatnesse? Either to harbour fled,
Or made a Toste for Neptune.

Such a passage as this, with its heroic exaggeration
and Polonian antithesis, bridges the gap between

oratory and sententiousness, showing Agamemnon to be more akin to Gonzalo than to Hector.

The exuberance of Coriolanus' friend, Menenius, in verse, and even more in prose, has close affinities with that of Nestor. Such a decked-out proverb as:

> This Tiger-footed-rage, when it shall find
> The harme of unskan'd swiftnesse will (too late)
> Tye Leaden pounds too's heeles,

is quite in the manner of the over-wise Greek. But Menenius is too much of a conscious buffoon to be classed with the stock councillors, whose humour lies largely in their own humourlessness.

The chief examples of the type are Polonius, Gonzalo, and perhaps Brabantio. Antigonus, so long as he is Antigonus, is of them too, as revealed in his comically ogreish plans for his daughters, and the "La you now" with which he gives in to his wife; but for the most part he is only an instrument for the depositing of Perdita with proper impressiveness in Bohemia, and there forgets his character in his office. In all these councillors exaggeration has become periphrasis, and the boast turned to the proverb. The kinship of these two modes has been already noticed, and, though Polonius' verse cannot be called bombastic, his formality and tediousness is nevertheless a direct descendant of the bombast of self-importance. With his long-winded periods in mind, it is easier to analyse the peculiar verse-flavour of Caesar and Agamemnon.

The same connection, between bombast and formality, is again apparent in the speech of Gloucester in *Lear*. He shows at once by his courtly loquacity, his superstition, and his pathetic trustfulness that he is of the old coun-cillor breed. His fussy exclamations, when ex-cited, recall Brabantio:

Kent banish'd thus? and France in choller parted?
And the King gone tonight? Prescrib'd his powre,
Confin'd to exhibition? All this done
Upon the gad? Edmund, how now? What newes?

and again:

O Villain, villain: his very opinion in the Letter. Abhorred Villaine, unnaturall, detested, brutish Vil-laine; worse then brutish: Go sirrah, seeke him: Ile apprehend him. Abhominable Villaine, where is he?

By the time that the scene of the putting out of his eyes is reached, he should be firmly estab-lished as a comic character; so that the lamentings of the critics, that Shakspere should so far have bowed to the tastes of his age as to put this spectacle of revolting cruelty upon the stage, are largely uncalled for. It seems to me much more likely that the Elizabethan audience received it with howls of encouragement and delight than with gasps even of gratified horror. The tortured Gloucester is much nearer to the long-suffering Pantaloon of Harlequinade, or the old horse disembowelled in the bull-fight, than to a tragic martyr.

This is clear from the scene itself, quite apart from Gloucester's previous record, examined above. There is something comic alike in the energy of his persecutors and in the pomposity of his defiance, pathetic as it is. It is indeed necessary to the plan of the play that it should be so. In *Lear*, as in *Hamlet*, the main story is echoed in the underplot; and as the tragedy of Lear himself contains elements of the grotesque, it is imperative that Gloucester's agony should be kept well under control, lest it should appear the more tragic of the two.

Here the "tedious old fool", under the stress of great emotion, moderates naturally to bombast. Gloucester's final defiance contains all the stock ingredients: the monster-suggestion in "boarish phangs", hell, a tempest hyperbole, wild conditionals—"would have, should'st have"—and the strained description of Lear's weeping as "he holpe the heavens to raine".

This use of bombast, to suggest the taint of pomposity, is not confined to the aged statesmen. In this same play is so portrayed the "moral fool" in Albany. Listening to his righteous indignation, an audience can sympathise at once with Albany's justness, and Gonerill's scorn and impatience, as she says "No more; the text is foolish". With this, the formality of courts— Duncan and Vincentio are guilty; the prolixity of age, as in Antony's tutor, and the old man with whom Ross discusses the storm at Duncan's death; the self-consciousness of the shy—neither Troilus nor Cordelia is wholly exempt; all these are variants of that lack of spontaneity which Shakspere so often makes manifest as bombast.

It is at this point that the examination definitely enters upon dangerous ground. An Elizabethan audience, brought up on Marlowe and Kyd and their successors, and with a natural worship of energy and enthusiasm, would have recognised without a doubt the heroic, the regal, and the sententious indications of bombast. But these subtle hints of insincerity—even with Jonson's testimony that they were ready to recognise false and fusty stuff and to condemn it —would the Elizabethans have understood them? I think myself that they did; the examples themselves prove it. But the question is all the more important now, when proceeding to the consideration of two kinds of deliberate insincerity, which seem both to have been portrayed by bombast—namely forced rages and false rows.

Anger is a passion which, for all its multiplicity of cause and kind, varies little in its actual manifestations. The hysterical man, and he who, like Homer's lion and Longinus' Euripides, lashes himself to fury, make much the same grimaces; and oaths and hyperboles serve equally well as spur and safety-valve. The variety of angry men which Shakspere produces, through his command of differing rhythms and verse-qualities, is therefore remarkable. The surge and thunder of Lear's apostrophes is quite different from the sudden frenzy of Othello, or Antony's almost lyrical cries of anguish; while the elaborately monstrous images of Cleopatra's rage bear no likeness to the broken curses of Leontes. Here it is necessary to consider only those whose anger appears unreasonably vehement, who, whether by nature or design, deliberately force their passion.

The choleric man, and more particularly the comically angry father, was a stock character of the Greek New Comedy and its Roman imitators. This humour, with the braggart soldier, was resurrected by the Elizabethans, but only Shakspere, after producing an orthodox specimen in Old Capulet, had the courage and skill to make of the buffoon a tragic hero.

Lear, in the early scenes of the play, is true to type. The tragedy must arise from the unreasonableness of his passion, and Lear is accordingly shown deliberately indulging it, goading himself on with oaths and apostrophes, and extravagant pictures of the barbarous Scythians or the sea-monster. As Dr Johnson remarks, upon his swearing by Jupiter: "Shakspere makes his Lear too much a mythologist; he had Hecate and Apollo before." He has more to come; in the scene with Gonerill he calls upon darkness and devils, life and death, and apostrophises ingratitude, himself, Cordelia's fault, nature, blasts, fogs, and his own eyes; later still there are Juno, vengeance plague death and confusion in

[ 131 ]          9-2

a single line, breath and blood, death on his state, and numerous curses. But already, in the wonderful little scene between Lear and the fool, as they wait for the horses to be saddled, a change of method is apparent. The mutterings of this scene are echoed in the horrible inarticulate mouthings into which Lear falls when Regan too proves ungrateful. With this the comedy is broken; with a shock the supposed joke is found to be in deadly earnest. Henceforth, though the apostrophes grow wilder and more tremendous, there are no more strange oaths, and the hints and mutterings become commoner, until the hysterical verse froths over into the prose of a broken mind.

After Lear, Shakspere created another choleric father in Cymbeline; but his rage, confined to one short scene, is puny beside that of the other British King, and consists largely of that singularly mild abuse so common in the late plays. Much closer to Lear's fury are the curses of Timon.

Judgments upon *Timon of Athens* must be uncertain, since it is probable that Shakspere would not have regarded the present play as complete. The two Timons, before, and after, disillusionment, have no connection with each other; yet the second, as choler personified, will bear comparison with the typically choleric man of the early Lear.

The two are strikingly alike in their frenzy, whether from design, or merely because they are contemporaries. Timon's first speech without the walls of Athens, as Lear's outside Gloucester's castle, is an unbroken string of thunderous apostrophes and curses. But whereas with Lear this is the final outburst, carefully prepared and introduced, with Timon it occurs after a lightning change of character, and his sudden madness appears unnatural. The blame for this may be laid either on the fact that the second Timon is little more than a mouthpiece, a Morality character "Misanthropy"; or upon the imperfect state of the play and the consequent unrevised abruptness of the transition. The exaggeration of Timon's speech has obviously no dramatic purpose.

In considering the false notes of Lear's anger mention was made of the horrors with which he tortures his imagination:

> The barbarous Scythian,
> Or he that makes his generation messes

> To gorge his appetite, shall to my bosome
> Be as well neighbour'd, pittied, and releev'd
> As thou my sometime Daughter.

This is also Cleopatra's chief device for the sustaining of her acted rages. When told of Antony's marriage to Octavia she invents torments for the messenger, cries:

> Melt Egypt into Nyle; and kindly creatures
> Turne all to Serpents,

and when the wretched messenger asks "should I lye, Madame?" replies:

> Oh, I would thou didst:
> So halfe my Egypt were submerg'd and made
> A Cesterne for scal'd Snakes.

Her rage at being outwitted and finally captured by Caesar's soldiers is no less extravagant, so that Proculeius remarks primly:

> You do extend
> These thoughts of horror further than you shall
> Finde cause in *Caesar*.

There is, of course, no reason to suppose that Cleopatra is not deeply and sincerely angry at these moments. But it is obvious that she indulges the passion, and takes pleasure in goading herself to further lengths. The spur can be felt

in such phrases as "a CESTERNE for SCAL'D SNAKES"
or "Rather on Nylus' mudde Lay me STARKE-
NAK'D, and let the water-flies, BLOW me into
abHORING". And there is the same movement,
fluent and yet strongly stressed, in her more
deliberate passions, as:

Why should I thinke you can be mine, and true,
(Though you in swearing shake the Throaned Gods),
Who have been false to Fulvia?

where emphasis is aided both by exaggeration
and alliteration; and the still more amazing:

SINKE ROME and THEIR TONGUES ROT
That speake against us.

These regular lines with forced extravagant
stresses give the impression of a past-mistress in
the art of making a scene, who uses her technique
to improve even her genuine rages. Whether
Shakspere conceived her, like Othello, as an
Oriental, and how far her extravagance is due
ultimately to this cause, is an interesting problem. Her followers and attendants certainly
elaborate their speech to a greater degree than is
usual with the normal courts which Shakspere
models on the English; and their exuberance very
probably symbolises eastern luxury.

Cleopatra is Shakspere's masterpiece of insincerity; Troilus one of the most sincere persons he ever drew. Yet Troilus' rage upon Cressida's betrayal, though of a quality very different from Cleopatra's, is nevertheless strangely unconvincing. Omitting his perhaps conventional asides—"O plague and madnesse", "by hell and all hell's torments", "wert thou the divell..."—consider the following speeches, in which he attempts to dissuade his senses, then vows vengeance:

> ...this is, and is not *Cressid*.
> Within my soule, there doth conduce a fight
> Of this strange nature, that a thing inseparate
> Divides more wider than the skie and earth:
> And yet the spacious bredth of this division
> Admits no Orifex for a point as subtle,
> As Ariachne's broken woof to enter:
> Instance, O instance! strong as Plutoe's gates:
> Cressid is mine, tied with the bonds of heaven;
> Instance, O instance, strong as heaven itselfe:
> The bonds of heaven are slipt, dissolved and loos'd...

and again:

> that shall be divulged well
> In Characters as red as *Mars* his heart
> Inflam'd with Venus....
> That Sleeve is mine, that heele beare in his helme:
> Were it a Caske compos'd by Vulcan's skill,

My Sword should bite it: Not the dreadfull spout,
Which Shipmen doe the Hurricano call,
Constring'd in masse by the almighty Sunne,
Shall dizzie with more clamour Neptune's eare
In his discent; then shall my prompted sword
Falling on Diomed....
O Cressid! O false Cressid! false, false, false:
Let all untruths stand by thy stained name
And theyle seeme glorious.

The whole of this passage, from the cold-blooded balance of the opening to the bombastic threats and ranted regrets of the end, seems to me wearily unnatural; hitherto Troilus has appeared as an affected lover, a self-conscious wooer, and a somewhat flamboyant idealist, but there has been no forecast of this strange, posing desperation, in which he continues for the rest of the play.

"For th' love of all the gods", he cries to Hector:

Let's leave the Hermit Pitty with our Mothers:
And when we have our Armour buckled on,
The venom'd vengeance ride upon our swords:

and later, more petulantly still:

                        Who should withhold me?
Not fate, obedience, nor the hand of *Mars*
Beckning with fierie trunchion my retire.

Thence to the battle-brag of the last scenes, which have been rejected by so many critics as non-Shaksperian. It would be an easy way out of the difficulty thus to condemn the whole act; but however much or little Shakspere wrote of it himself, there can, I think, be traced throughout these scenes a design, and a method of carrying out that design, which is eminently Shaksperian, and appears in others of the tragedies. The combination of bombast and rhymed couplets creates a sense of futility remaining after the catastrophe comparable with that which comes with the final couplets of *King Lear*, or, more fleetingly, with the bombast of *Macbeth*, and of *Antony and Cleopatra*. Troilus' unnaturalness, then, is not intended to throw any light upon himself or his own personality; it is rather an expression of that desperate world-weariness which Cleopatra states, more concisely perhaps, but not more successfully, in her lament:

Oh wither'd is The Garland of the Warre,
The Souldiers pole is falne: young Boys and Gyrles
Are levell now with men: The oddes is gone
And there is nothing left remarkable
Beneath the visiting Moone.

Another example of extravagance, which is to

[ 138 ]

a large extent independent of character, is found
in the bombast of Laertes. Allowance, of course,
must be made for the fact that he is of the warrior
type, a horseman and a "sworder", straightforward and yet hard, a Claudio or a Bertram
rather than a Coriolanus. When he heads a rebellion to avenge his father's death, he is
heroically pugnacious:

> How came he dead? Ile not be Juggel'd with.
> To hell Allegeance: Vowes, to the blackest divell.
> Conscience and Grace to the profoundest Pit.
> I dare Damnation:

but at the burial of Ophelia his bombast is less
convincing:

> Hold off the earth awhile,
> Till I have caught her once more in my armes:
> Now pile your dust, upon the quicke, and dead,
> Till of this flat a Mountaine you have made
> To o're top old Pelion, or the skyish head
> Of blew *Olympus*.

The suddenness of his outburst, and the
elaborate sonority of his periods, ring false. The
situation here is very close to that of Gloucester
in *Lear*. Laertes' tragedy echoes Hamlet's, as
Gloucester's does that of Lear; Hamlet himself,
though he rates himself for cursing like a drab,

has no passage in this extravagant style of bombast. His most highly coloured verse occurs when his play has succeeded, and he goes to interview that mother, whose sin is the origin of his horror and agony:

'Tis now the verie witching time of night,
When Churchyards yawne, and Hell itselfe breaths out
Contagion to this world. Now could I drink hot blood,
And do such bitter businesse as the day
Would quake to looke on. Soft now, to my mother,

and this genuine agitation continues throughout the scene in Gertrude's chamber. Laertes' passion must recall Hamlet's own, but in no way surpass it. It is therefore made slightly ridiculous, and its unnaturalness is emphasised by Hamlet's hysterical parody of it. Though it does reveal Laertes' commonplace and conventional character, its main dramatic purpose is to show Hamlet's own advance from desperation to a state of comparative detachment, in which he can detect and condemn another's extravagance.

Insincerity of a vow or protestation can be suggested in the same way as insincerity of passion. Critics have already claimed one example of this in Macbeth's grief and clamour upon Duncan's death:

DONAL. What is amisse?
MACB.                    You are, and doe not know't:
The Spring, the Head, the Fountaine of your Blood
Is stopt, the very Source of it is stopt,

and more particularly the line

Here lay *Duncan*
His Silver skinne, lac'd with his Golden Blood,

which has been seized upon as the height of extravagance and falsity. Some have even found a further subtlety in the sharp word "lac'd", with its suggestion of punctures, revealing the true horror which the sight of the "gash'd Stabs" he made has produced in the mind of the dissembling murderer. But changes of word-association have made this passage more striking than it deserves. A modern writer could hardly choose less apt epithets for skin and blood than the hard, metallic, essentially inorganic, "silver" and "gold"; and "lac'd" with its connection boots and bodices, may now legitimately call up images of blood pricking from punctured holes. But to the Elizabethans gold was red-gold, and silver was the stock adjective, for, among other things, swans; while "lac'd", so far from suggesting punctures, was a synonym for "embroidered" in its most general and least technical sense. Eyelids are "lac'd" with blue veins, and there is the striking phrase in Shakspere's sixty-seventh sonnet:

> Sin by him advantage should achieve
> And lace itselfe with his society,

where the word seems merely to mean "adorn", "deck itself out". The nearest approach to a puncture association are the whores' backs "laced" with lashes; but even here the weals are considered more as a work of art than as a torture.

The offending line then would not have been so markedly outstanding to an Elizabethan audience. And it is in any case inconsistent to blame Macbeth, while passing over the infinitely more extravagant outburst of Macduff.

This digression may perhaps be excused as an example of how uncertain all assessments of bombastic passages must be. There are, however, plenty of protesters who cannot be acquitted so easily as Macbeth. Shakspere's arch-cozener Iago, for instance, though for the most part he prefers

[ 142 ]

to work by hints and seeming honesty, yet employs these tactics for the last assault. "If thou dost slander her...", cries Othello, and his deceiver is full of righteous indignation, exclamations, apostrophes, and sententious couplets. And in the following narrative he becomes for once picturesque, and utters such phrases as:

> As if he pluckt up kisses by the rootes,
> That grew upon my lippes.

The climax comes with Othello's vow "by yond marble heaven" to be revenged. Iago falls on his knees beside him and swears also; but whereas Othello's oath was magnificent, Iago's imitation is overdone:

> Witnesse you ever-burning Lights above,
> You elements that clip us round about,
> Witnesse that here *Iago* doth give up
> The execution of his wit, hands, heart
> To wrong'd *Othello's* Service.

This bombast has a double effect; it shows Iago both over-emphasising his feigned loyalty, and maliciously caricaturing his general at the same time.

Another example comes from Cymbeline.

Iachimo, in his first attempt upon Imogen, combines Iago's hints with protestations:

What, are men mad? Hath Nature given them eyes
To see this vaulted Arch, and the rich Crop
Of Sea and Land, which can distinguish 'twixt
The firie Orbes above, and the twinn'd Stones
Upon the number'd Beach, and can we not
Partition make with Spectacles so pretious
Twixt faire, and foule?

and

Lamentable: what!
To hide me from the radiant Sun, and solace
I' th' Dungeon by a Snuffe!

Here the suggestion of falsity by exaggeration may seem, as in the poet's flattery of the fallen Timon, too obvious to remark upon; and the same is true of the deceits of the bad people in *Lear*, although these, held back by their natural coldness of disposition, are never wild in protestation. Their bombast is rather that of thought than of language or movement. Gonerill, indeed, is no more extravagant than many of Shakspere's most sincere avowers:

Sir, I love you more then word can weild the matter,
Deerer then eye-sight, space, and libertie,
etc. etc.

in Regan's speech the false note is more easily detected:

> I professe
> My selfe an enemy to all other joyes,
> Which the most precious square of sense possesses,
> And find I am alone felicitate
> In your deere Highnesse love,

while Edmund is quite exuberant in inventing Edgar's assault upon him:

> In fell motion
> With his prepared Sword, he charges home
> My unprovided body, latch'd mine arme;
> And when he saw my best alarum'd spirits
> Bold in the quarrels right, rouz'd to th' encounter,
> Or whether gasted by the noyse I made,
> Full sodainely he fled.

This fluent *Henry V* stuff stands out strikingly from the more wrought and mature verse which surrounds it.

Something of this same openness and shamelessness of deceit (though it is all more subtly done) is present in the avowals of love with which Cleopatra keeps Antony by her side. It has been already noticed that the tone of conversation in the Egyptian court is forced and unnatural, and that the Queen herself enjoys extravagance. This is even more obvious in the two great scenes in which Cleopatra protests her loyalty to her lover. In the first of these Antony discovers her in the act of betraying him to Caesar's emissary. There is a scene: Antony, half-hysterical in his desperation, blurts out all the bitter truths of Cleopatra's harlotry, which he has always known, but hitherto repressed. The Queen's interjections show her completely unashamed; "Oh, is't come to this?" she says, "Wherefore is this?" and "Have you done yet?" But he has not done; "I must stay his time", says Cleopatra composedly, and a moment later Antony, with "Cold-hearted toward me?" gives her the chance she has been waiting for. She is prompt to take the cue:

> Ah (Deere) if I be so,
> From my cold heart let Heaven ingender haile,
> And poyson it in the sourse, and the first stone
> Drop in my necke: as it determines so
> Dissolve my life, the next *Caesarion* smite,
> Till by degrees the memory of my wombe,
> Together with my brave Egyptians all,
> By the discandying of this pelleted storme,
> Lye gravelesse, till the Flies and Gnats of Nyle
> Have buried them for prey.

This must be without exception the most

monstrously unconvincing protestation in Shakspere, even without Cleopatra's previous self-possession to throw it into yet greater relief. It appears that Antony too is aware of the deceit, as he succumbs to it; for with a brief "I am satisfied", he turns hurriedly to the business of the war. As he does so he realises that all is not yet lost, and his hysterical resolution changes suddenly to a courage equally strained and desperate; and so the scene closes.

Compare with this Cleopatra's behaviour at Antony's death. Antony, dying, with a bungled wound in the stomach, is carried before the Queen, high in her monument. She calls aloud on the sun to be darkened, but hastily refuses to come down to her lover, lest she herself be captured. Antony is, however, eventually hoisted up to her, and there seeks to gasp out his last words of advice and consolation. But even now, with her lover dying miserably before her, she cannot be sincere. "No, let me speake", she cries, and launches into the fulsome oration appropriate to the occasion; and when Antony, desperately breaking through, in pain and agony utters his advice, she curtly rejects the interruption. The scene is ludicrous; and it is, I am sure, intended to be so. The sense of tragic futility and wasted effort, so strong throughout the play, here reaches its climax.

It is interesting to examine in detail the speeches of Cleopatra at the opening of this scene. The first is a Senecan apostrophe:

> Oh Sunne,
> Burne the great Sphere thou mov'st in, darkling
> stand
> The varrying shore o' th' world.

Shortly after this comes a highly artificial triplet in the Kyd style:

> if Knife, Drugges, Serpents have
> Edge, sting, or operation, I am safe.

A classical allusion follows, and Seneca completes the circle with an hyperbole:

> let me rayle so hye,
> That the false Huswife, Fortune, breake her Wheele,
> Provok'd by my offence.

When Antony dies she seems at last to give way to genuine feeling, and even resolves to accompany her lover in his suicide "after the high Roman fashion". But in the next act she is still calling magnificently upon death, while secretly making arrangements for the reservation of her fortune, and pumping susceptible Roman officers as to the chances of escape. Note that here Shakspere makes one of his widest divergences from Plutarch. According to the Life, Cleopatra, having wounded herself in her passionate lamentation over the dead Antony, betakes herself to her bed in a state of collapse, and there receives the asp. The play shows her perfectly self-possessed to the last, committing suicide with an air of nobility certainly, yet only because her protestations have at last proved unable to save her from disgrace.

With Cleopatra's behaviour in mind, it is surprising to discover that the language of Cressida, her rival, if a weak one, is on the whole natural and unaffected; more so, indeed, than that of Troilus, who, being the stock Elizabethan lover, is full of furnace sighs and elaborate comparisons. In the first scene he has already cried:

> O that her Hand
> (In whose comparison, all whites are Inke,
> Writing their owne reproach;)

called upon Apollo to tell him

> for thy *Daphnes* Love
> What *Cressid* is, what *Pandar*, and what we:

and found the answer, apparently, in an elaborate
simile. When he woos, he is "giddy; expectation
whirles him round", and he betrays his shyness
in the affected prose already mentioned. Whereas
the only speech-evidence for Cressida's falsehood
are her sinister couplet-sequences, which have
been discussed above, and this one patch of bombast:

O you gods divine!
Make *Cressid's* name the very crowne of falshood!
If ever she leave *Troylus*: time, force, and death,
Do to this body what extremes you can;
But the strong base and building of my love,
Is as the very Center of the earth,
Drawing all things to it. I will goe in and weepe,
Teare my bright heire, and scratch my praised cheekes.
Cracke my cleere voyce with sobs, and breake my
    heart
With sounding Troylus.

and again:

Why tell you me of moderation?

It cannot be to persuade Troilus of her loyalty
that she does this. Her only audience is her
knowing uncle and pander, who is not well cast
for the part of dupe. The effect of this protestation
depends largely on the spectator's knowledge of
the story, and awareness of the coming reversal

of Cressida's vows. But a case might also be made out for believing that she herself is equally aware of it, and is here trying to reassure herself with a passionate outburst, as before she has done, and later will do again, with proverbial couplets. Cressida would then be, not the stock harlot type, but a sketch for a character which was later, in Macbeth and Antony, to fascinate Shakspere: the man faced with a temptation, knowing, and desperate in the knowledge, that his fall is both fatal and inevitable. The apologist for Cressida would have to plead that in her case the plot is not fully or coherently worked out; that the drive of the main action demands that her fall should be unconvincingly sudden, and yet not more so than that of Timon, or even Othello.

It is more probable, however, that dramatic irony, the playing upon the spectator's fore-knowledge of events—and the story of Cressida, remember, was a mediaeval classic—is the chief purpose behind this speech; the effect is inde-pendent of Cressida's personal character. The critic cannot expect bombast, any more than prose, to be always an indication of the per-sonality or state of mind of the speaker. Examples have already been quoted in which it is employed to throw light upon the character of some other person, notably the glorification of warriors through the praises of their associates. Nor is it only warriors who are so raised; Enobarbus' famous description of Cleopatra—carefully placed in the middle of her longest disappearance from the stage—surrounds her with a glamour that no acting or staging could produce. And Cassio does the same service for Desdemona, when he presents her as a divinity whom even the forces of Nature will not harm. There are also innumerable hybrids, purple patches which magnify a character as well as perform some other function: Caesar's speech to Octavia, glorifying Antony while it reveals himself; and Imogen's lamentation over the headless body which she supposes Posthumus:

> this is his Hand:
> His Foote Mercuriall: his martiall Thigh
> The brawnes of *Hercules*: but his Jovial face—

and again: Damn'd *Pisanio*...hath...

> From this most bravest vessel of the world
> Strooke the maine top;

a combination of the heroic puff and the convention of horror.

A flight of conscious poetry is as useful in the

painting of scenes as in the dressing up of characters. A physical storm, or the coming of darkness, are favourite devices of Shakspere for the creation of a state of high emotional tension. Elizabethan stage resources were, however, limited; their thunder and lightning were crude imitations of the kettle-drum and fire-work kind, and their night-effects non-existent, at least in the unroofed public theatres. Shakspere was therefore forced to reproduce them in words, through the human reaction to them. Thus the opening of the second act of *Julius Caesar* combines the tempest and the night motifs. Casca's fulsome relation to Cicero of the storm, and its prodigies seen flaring through the darkness, prepares that strange thundery suspense which broods over Brutus' lightning-lit deliberation in the next scene.

A more subtle use of the device, here again in the form of a storm-description, is found in the second act of *Othello*. While Othello and Desdemona are still at sea, there is a great storm, described by a Cypriot gentleman in words already quoted:

For do but stand upon the Foaming Shore,
The chidden Billow seems to pelt the Clowds,

The winde-shak'd Surge, with high and monstrous
   Maine,
Seemes to cast water on the burning Beare,
And quench the Guards of th' ever-fixed Pole.

The deliberate monstrosity of this description
serves a double purpose; like the appearance of
the gentleman with the bloody knife in *Lear*, it
puts the audience into a state of suspense, and the
relief from this, in the safe arrival of both Desdemona and Othello, creates a sense of security
from which the final fall is the more disastrous;
and it also helps to give to Cyprus that character
of "a town of warre, Yet wilde, the people's
hearts brimfull of feare", which it is necessary it
should bear for the quarrel scene.

   Lear's appearance on the heath is also carefully prepared for by an extravagant storm-
picture. Before he himself is seen, his plight is
told to Kent by a Gentleman, in these words:

KENT.             Where's the King?
  GENT. Contending with the fretfull Elements,
Bids the winde blow the Earth into the Sea,
Or swell the curled Waters 'bove the Maine,
That things might change or cease; teares his white
   heire,
Which the impetuous Blasts, with eyeless rage,

Catch in their Fury, and make nothing of;
Strives in his little world of man to out-scorn
The to-and-fro-conflicting Winde and Rain.

This elaborate description shares with Lear's in-coherence, already mentioned, the responsibility for the extraordinary leap in emotional pitch between the second and third acts.

Often this verbal scene-painting is used to stimulate emotions less concrete and definite, to create in the audience merely a state of expectancy or receptivity. Of this kind were the passages already noted in *A Midsummer Night's Dream*, and probably also the lyrical interchange between Lorenzo and Jessica ("On such a night") in the last act of *The Merchant of Venice*, with Lorenzo's discourse on the stars and on music. To this preparation is largely due the dying fall of this play's last scene, so much more smooth and satisfying than the unravelings of the other comedies. It is, however, the tragedy of *Macbeth* which shows this use of bombast on the largest scale. Many critics have noticed a distinction between this and the other plays; it has been variously characterised as the most unreal, the most Senecan, and the most mutilated of Shak-spere's works. There is certainly a curious duality

[ 155 ]

in the verse. Purely dramatic lines, of the intensely vigorous and dynamic kind which Shakspere was then writing, alternate with the deliberately poetical, sustained recitations of the Senecan tradition.

An admirable example is the famous dagger speech. The first sixteen lines are dramatic; they depend largely for their effect upon the actor who gives them utterance, and lose considerably in reading. With "Now ore the one half-world Nature seems dead", there comes a complete change. This second half of the soliloquy is pure Senecan description; the images and emotions which it calls up are quite independent of the actor, who has no personal interest in them, becoming a mere mouthpiece for their delivery.

Even more striking are the two appearances of Banquo's ghost at the feast, which, with their similar introduction and totally dissimilar treatment, form a strange doublet. The purely dramatic reaction to the first shock, in the awful quietness of "Which of you hath done this?" contrasts oddly with the later screaming bravado of the conventional ghost-seer:

Avaunt, and quit my sight...
Approach thou like the rugged Russian Beare,

The arm'd Rhinoceros, or the Hyrcan Tyger,
Take any shape but that, and my firme Nerves
Shall never tremble, etc.

There is no need to seek any special external
cause for this unique treatment. The subject is
itself unique. The Senecan overlay in this play
is presumably a deliberate, certainly a successful, device to preserve the weird atmosphere of
suspense overshadowing Holinshed's haunted
tyrant. These strange impersonal asides suggest
at once the hysterical tension in the speaker, and
the brooding of the supernatural powers that
menace him. The tragedy of *Macbeth* is both a
model of ghost-story technique and a striking
study in the psychology of hysteria. From the
very opening Macbeth is

> ...one, that on a lonesome road
> Doth walk in fear and dread;
> And having once turned round walks on
> And turns no more his head;
> Because he knows, a frightful fiend
> Doth close behind him tread.

Apart from the supernatural introduction, the
highly coloured narrative of the bloody sergeant
—another "non-Shaksperian" passage—gives
the impression that Macbeth is fey even before his

dealings with the weird sisters. There is something uncanny in his desperate courage:

> Except they meant to bathe in reeking Wounds,
> Or memorize another *Golgotha*,
> I cannot tell.

Throughout the play bombast continues to create this sense of unnatural, frantic energy. The exaggerated clamour, both of men and of the elements, upon Duncan's death, has been already mentioned; Lady Macbeth is full of invocations which suggest the Black Mass; the tortured voice of Macbeth himself, rising hysterically higher and higher, is admirably shown in the strange crescendo of lyrical similes for sleep (yet another borrowing from the Sonneteers), where the final snapping of the nerves is only prevented by Lady Macbeth's tight-lipped "What do you meane?" And even in the last act the same method is preserved in the alternation between Macbeth's mad cries and the terrible quiet of his musings.

Macbeth, I have said, is unique. Shakspere never again required that atmosphere of brooding suspense which is here so well represented by the Senecan descriptions. The method can however be paralleled in many another passage where bombast is introduced expressly to play upon the nerves of the audience. And in that office it is the most powerful of all Shakspere's verse-effects.

# CONCLUSION

"SHAKSPEAR wanted Arte", declared Ben Jonson; and many subsequent critics, both friend and foe, have confirmed or admitted this judgment. I hope that the foregoing study of some of Shakspere's aims and methods has shown that he in fact possessed a great deal of art. If it has also revealed something of the kind and quality of that art, I have achieved my full purpose; what follows will be only elucidation and emphasis.

Jonson was, of course, a classicist; and in his judgment he was applying to Shakspere's work the classical criteria which he courted in his own. The complacency of our teachers may often have obscured the fallacy which underlies any such procedure: "Shakspere was a great dramatist", they tell us, "Ben Jonson a good one, but not so good as Shakspere, Chapman less good still, Beaumont-and-Fletcher, for all his former reputation, rather poor"; and so we are apt to ignore the fact that these so-called fellow-dramatists had each a totally distinct conception of drama. There can be no comparison between them.

It is always a difficult business to cram a large and vigorous living creature into a nutshell; the attempt may, however, emphasise the difference between the tiger, the elephant, and the shrew-mouse. Beaumont and Fletcher, then, were first and foremost masters of "good theatre"; to achieve the most tremendous stage-effects, that was their aim, and to that all else was sacrificed. Situations and characters are presented by them in as exaggerated a form as possible, that the clashes may be the more resounding; and their poetry bids as baldly for the softer effects as their dramatisation for the more striking. Chapman, on the other hand, a classicist like Jonson, neglected stage-effect. He was interested not in the changes and chances of action, but in their overtones, in the human thoughts and emotions resulting from them. Chapman's drama was Sophoclean, but without the vigorous roots of action upon which Sophocles founded his own. In such a play as *Byron* the action is astonishingly unimportant; the hero's intrigues—or is he the villain?—are forgotten in the philosophical and emotional reactions which are somehow derived from them. Jonson is another who preferred a play of thought. His motto was "Words above action, matter above words". And yet Jonson's plays are of a different type again from Chapman's. If Chapman's are Sophoclean, Jonson's are Aristophanic, whatever his opinion of Aristophanes himself. Jonson is a moralist, and he expresses his moral by forcing human life into a satirical pattern; his most original plays are therefore deliberately monotonous, with all illogicalities, inconsistencies, incompatibilities, filed down to fit in with his scheme.

Shakspere was different again. He was not concerned primarily with writing "good theatre", for all his time-serving; nor was he a moralist, whatever our great-grandfathers made of him. While he studied above all the overtones of action, he possessed no narrow scheme, moral or artistic, by which they were to be regulated. There is only one aim in his work: to present, as purely, as intensely, as elementally as possible, the tangle of human relations and interrelations with the thoughts and emotions struck out by them. To this aim all his resources, dramatisation, characterisation, poetry, are subservient.

It is always possible to dissect Shakspere's

work and find fault with the parts; to apply a rule to his morals, his dramatic construction, or his poetry, and to declare, with Jonson, that the first is ridiculous, the second irregular, and the third uneven. But that is to neglect the power of combination. Criticism to-day, studious of the poet's technical achievement, has managed to forget Shakspere the philosopher and Shakspere the psychologist; yet it still tends to split up the remainder into Shakspere the poet and Shakspere the dramatist. His use of words and of imagery has been examined; research into the conditions of the Elizabethan stage has revealed some of the physical conventions which helped and hindered him as a playwright. All this, however, is not enough. Shakspere was neither a pure poet, nor a simple dramatist, but a combination of the two. Not the *Venus and Adonis*, nor the *Lucrece*, not the *Sonnets*, nor the *Phoenix and the Turtle*, nor even an anthology of all the famous set-pieces from the plays, could have in themselves given to Shakspere that place which he holds as a poet. And for his claims as a working dramatist, it must be admitted that both Marston and Middleton were his equals in the invention of striking situations (with the added distinction of composing their plots themselves), and that the prize for mastery of purely stage-effect goes to the firm of Beaumont and Fletcher. Shakspere is supreme only as a dramatic poet; as a Janus, in a better sense than that in which Dryden bestowed the name. For his poetic attention is always bent upon his dramatisation, his dramatic upon his poetry. And if we too, in studying Shakspere's work, could more often achieve this two-faced attitude, could examine his drama with a poet's eye and his poetry with a dramatist's, there would be less either of Jonsonian fault-finding or of trespassing that side idolatry.

For EU product safety concerns, contact us at Calle de José Abascal, 56–1°, 28003 Madrid, Spain or eugpsr@cambridge.org.